BEYOND THE OUIJA BOARD

A WWII Teenager In Occupied Belgium

Arlette deMonceau Michaelis

Edited by Maryann McLoughlin O'Donnell, Ph. D.
A project of the Holocaust Resource Center
The Richard Stockton College of New Jersey

COMTEQ
PUBLISHING
MARGATE, NEW JERSEY

Published by:
    ComteQ Publishing
    A division of ComteQ Communications, LLC
    P.O. Box 3046
    Margate, New Jersey 08402
    609-487-9000 • Fax 609-822-4098
    Email: publisher@ComteQcom.com
    Website: www.ComteQpublishing.com

ISBN 0-9674074-9-4
Library of Congress Control Number: 2005921927

Book design by Rob Huberman
Cover design by Jacob Pezzicola
OUIJA® & ©2004 Hasbro, Inc. Used with permission.

Printed in the United States of America
10 9 8 7 6 5 4 3 2 1

Dedication

Mieux vaut mourir debout
Que vivre a genoux....
"*It is better to die on your feet than to live on your knees.*"—
attributed to Emiliano Zapata

To my parents whose faith in our allies' victory never faltered.

To my brothers and sister whose faith in my relating our tale never faltered.

To my children whose attention rarely faltered.

To my students whose memories of my stories seldom faltered.

To my husband Lansing whose health faltered and was unable to read this book before its publication.

Table of Contents

Preface

A rlette deMonceau Michaelis has been working on her book, *Beyond the Ouija Board: A WWII Teenager in Occupied Belgium,* * for nearly two years. The details in her memoir about World War II and the occupation of Belgium by the Nazis are impressive. During these years she was a teenager living in Brussels, Belgium, coping with the occupation and trying to help her family save Jews and fight the Nazis.

Years later, as a sixth grade teacher, Arlette told her story to many classes. By telling her story and answering students' questions she has remembered even more details of her life during the Nazi occupation of Belgium—for example, further details about her family's interaction with Jews and her family's efforts to hide and save Jews from deportation to concentration camps.

Readers will enjoy Arlette's stories of how her family solved many of the problems associated with the occupation. She makes solving these difficulties sound like fun; for example, she talks about there being no *How to Raise Rabbits for Dummies* back then or she talks about making a fire with a coal substitute. Under cover of her humor is the fact that Arlette was living in dangerous times, especially because she and her parents were hiding and helping Jews, and she and her brother were harassing Nazis every chance they could. When her parents and brother were imprisoned, she and her sister had to grow up quickly. Overnight they had to assume adult responsibilities.

Arlette's memoir is a window on the past, taking readers through the years of the war and its aftermath. Older readers will remember rationing, turning shirt collars, and mending silk hose. Younger readers will learn how teenagers of those years lived and coped—recognizing themselves in Arlette's stories of growing up, or coming of age.

All will be inspired by Arlette and her family who did whatever they could to resist the Nazis and fight for their freedom. The family were *upstanders,* a word coined by the well known journalist Samantha Power, to describe people who are not

bystanders but are instead people who seek to make a difference when others are being victimized.
Arlette deMonceau's *Beyond the Ouija Board: A WWII Teenager in Occupied Belgium* will be a pleasure for readers. Her story is inspiriting.

Dr. Maryann McLoughlin, Holocaust Resource Center, Richard Stockton College of New Jersey

Dr. Mary Johnson, Facing History and Ourselves Foundation

A note about the title:
Ouija is the trademark name of a board game, now made by Hasbro, Inc. There is a board with the alphabet and other signs on it. This is used with a planchette (a small triangular or heart-shaped board) to seek "spiritual or telepathic" messages. Arlette and her friends played with this during the war years.

Foreword

During my years as a school teacher (I was a sixth grade teacher, teaching everything except music and physical education), I realized that students were far more interested in my telling them about my war adventures than in hearing about the establishment of the border with Canada, the categories of Mexico's exports, or the third voyage of Christopher Columbus to the New World. I took my role as storyteller very seriously, and I proceeded to unveil my memories of being a teenager during World War II in Nazi-occupied Belgium. The students were fascinated by the tales and requested more details each time we met for Social Studies. Even now, when I meet my former students, they recall with clarity my rebellion against the Nazis but have forgotten the precious moments I spent teaching them about Torricelli and his fabulous air pressure experiments. Now they recall only my war stories with such precision and such minute details that even I have trouble remembering today.

I also found that my life as a teenager during the Nazi occupation had that special cachet which gave me the opportunity to connect with my students in a very concrete way. In giving them the opportunity to learn about my past, I was able to seize a part of my past when I shared my memories with my students.

For example, I came to view my parents in a different light, and the actions they had taken during the occupation of Belgium took on a new significance. All the accounts and books I had read about the war had mainly described famous battles and the strategies of the various armies as well as the political events that shaped that era. Then came the thousands of books relating the atrocities committed in the concentration camps during the Holocaust.

However, as my memories started to surface, I realized anew that I had had a part in a war that involved not only armies but civilians as well. This book relates the experiences of teenagers, how they kept their sanity, and how they dealt with adversity. I tried to make light of some events without resorting to cynicism and without ignoring the sufferings of so many victims. Young people have great resilience and have a knack of finding humor in most situations. Where I don't find humor are in my memories of the round up by the Nazis of young Belgians civilians as soon as they reached 18 yrs of age. Many of these Belgians died in labor camps in Europe. Neither do I find humor in my memories of the Jews persecuted by the Nazis. Those not hidden were deported and died in the concentration camps. These Belgians—Jews and non-Jews—were our dear friends.

I also realized how the war had changed the behavior of Belgian teens. By nature, teenagers are not patriotic, considering patriotism un-cool and a trait belonging to the old folks. This was not true during the war. We became patriots. As soon as the war was declared, patriotism surged through each and every one of us with great force.

School, which for most students was certainly not the place of choice, became fashionable, especially because it had been closed by the Kaiser during WWI. Young people were determined to continue their education, which now became as precious as the jewel in the king's crown.

As for the Church, it couldn't have opened its doors wide enough or fast enough. The agnostics of yore became fervent churchgoers not necessarily believers, probably to test the power of the Almighty. Yet I have to add that the greater number of the clergy conducted themselves like true saints with courage, dignity, and the self-denial.

Teenagers are by nature always hungry, and food plays an important role in their daily life. However, after food, teenagers have an immense desire for liberty. Teenagers despise curfews, rules, and regulations; they love to express their opinions openly regardless of the consequences. The Nazis deprived the Belgians of the freedom they cherished. But the loss of freedom took a graver toll on the rebellious younger population. The Belgians had fought for that right since 57 BCE when they battled Caesar who recognized their fierceness and described it so well in *Commentarii de bello Gallo* or *Gallic Wars*. Caesar said, "Of all the people in Gaul, the Belgians are the Bravest."

My intent in writing this book is to emphasize the importance of freedom of thought and the almost divine right given to all individuals to express it without restriction. For the basic need of self-preservation, food is necessary, but freedom is irreplaceable. Its only exchange is prison or death, and we understood this basic right, so during World War II, we defied our enemy at every turn. The Belgians are proud of their democratic ideals as well as their judicial ethics that the Nazis quickly destroyed. For in the Nazi regime the accused was always guilty and had to prove his or her innocence. This devious way to administer justice was the opposite of our judicial system in which the accuser has to prove the guilt of the accused beyond a reasonable doubt just as is the case in other democracies. This philosophy is really the cornerstone of my thoughts and a great emphasis, in my book, is put on that premise.

And now, dear readers, enjoy my book . . . .

A.M.

Prologue

The country of Belgium, unwillingly, became the World War I battlefield of Europe when German troops invaded that country on August 4, 1914. During the four-year occupation of Belgium, from August 1914 to November 1918, the German army terrorized the Belgian population and committed atrocities, slaughtering men, women, and children.

The Belgians were known for their patriotism, their courage, and their devotion to King Albert I (1875-1934), who fought the enemy with his soldiers. The king was the embodiment of Belgian idealism, the defender of the land and its patrimony, and the representative of the liberties of the democratic ideals and system of government.

The Allies joined forces to repel the invader and many of the battles took place in Belgium where civilians and soldiers fought fiercely side-by-side in order to defeat Europe's common enemy. The war ended in 1918 with the total defeat of Germany, but Belgium was in shambles. Thereafter the Belgians lived in fear of being invaded again; moreover, they had developed a deep-seated hatred of the Germans. Monuments erected to the memory of heroes and martyrs to this day pepper Belgium, France, England, and America. Stories of the cruelty of the enemy to the civilian population were told for years after the Allied victory but the country had rallied around their king, Albert I, who became an example of patriotism to his beloved subjects. He died in 1934 and was succeeded by his son Leopold III.

— CHAPTER ONE —

As It Was in the Beginning

In September 1939, at fifteen, I—Arlette deMonceau—was the oldest of three children. My brother Guy was fourteen years old, and my sister Ginette, twelve. My father was a civil engineer who at the onset of the war headed his own business in Brussels, Belgium. He assessed real estate properties with finesse and dexterity. He had a very sharp mind and loved to read. Well versed in history, he excelled in mathematics and was famous for his knack of turning a losing argument into a victory, a knack that many a time had infuriated my mother.

My father was born in 1898 and my mother in 1902 (although she claimed 1904 as her birth date). I adored my mother who was a petite woman with beautiful green eyes. She had the spirit of a tiger and was known to put her foot down when my father was contrary. She had been an excellent student and was well educated in music and the arts.

My parents, married in March 1923, were not rolling in money but had a prestigious name, which inspired respect from our peers. My ancestors, originally from France, had had titles (such as

Marquis) centuries ago. However, during the French Revolution
my ancestors fled France, leaving the title behind, and escaped to
Belgium, taking refuge as common citizens in Brussels.   My
parents demanded good manners and despised vulgarity. We lived
in a middle class neighborhood and always had had a car. My
father was impatient and couldn't waste his time waiting for a
streetcar, so a car was a necessity, he thought. Another necessity
was a nap; papa took a little nap every day right after lunch at
around 1:00 pm, so he organized his life around that time of day,
which became sacred as his life progressed. My mother was a
homemaker but had a cleaning lady who would do the heavier
chores once or twice a week.

— CHAPTER TWO —

The End of the Good Life

Unbeknownst to us, September 1939 marked the end of an
era of peace and relative prosperity. The tension buzzing
in the air was palpable. Everybody seemed to be on edge
not knowing what was going to happen. Germany was boiling and
the arrogance of Hitler didn't bode well. Papa told us the mood
and uncertainty we were experiencing was a repeat of the anxiety
Europe felt in 1914 just before World War I.

The signs that something strange was afoot were emphasized
by the crazy speeches of Hitler, the Fuhrer, always preceded by
military parades in the main German cities.   A constant
atmosphere of uncontained enthusiasm emanated from the
German youth. Huge crowds of uniformed men and women were
enthralled by the long-winded speeches of the Fuhrer. Flags lining
the wide avenues all over Germany and the overwhelming
enthusiasm of the crowds when Hitler spoke showed the world
that Germany was powerful and coming into her own after the
years of uncertainty and extreme poverty that the Germans
experienced after WWI and the punitive Versailles Treaty, which
demanded heavy reparations for the war. As a result, France and

England, who had always enjoyed a peaceful rivalry, became friendlier toward each other and started to rebuild the unity they had shared during WWI.

The Belgian king, Leopold III, was considered a pacifist. He said that he chose to remain neutral for fear of the country's being harassed by Germany. We didn't believe this. He remained neutral, some thought, because he was enthralled by the Nazis; after all, he was of German heritage and his sister was married to Humberto, an Italian prince in service to *Il Duce*, the Italian Fascist dictator, Benito Mussolini. Many suspected his sister had cautioned Leopold and in turn he feared for his throne. The French speaking Belgians didn't particularly love him; he gave many speeches in Flemish and seemed to have more affinity with the Flemish speaking Belgians than the others. However, I don't think he was openly pro German.

On September 1, 1939, even though school wasn't in session yet, we were summoned by our principal to attend the funeral of a beloved ex-Mayor of Brussels, Adolphe Max. Max, a hero of the World War I, was worshipped by the Brusselese for the front he presented to the *Boches* of 1914. (The Germans were called *Boches* during the World War I, 1914 – 1918.) Regarded as a great man and known to us kids as a wiry little Belgian with a neat haircut, silver hair and a little goatee, Max represented the embodiment of freedom and patriotism. During his funeral a surge of patriotism ran through our veins.

While we were attending his funeral, a sudden rush and movement of troops, mounted *gendarmes*—our Belgian state troopers—galloped all over the city. These powerful figures were in full uniform. I shall always remember the thundering noise of the horses' hooves on the cobblestones. The troopers' demeanor was serious. We were impressed and slightly scared. We couldn't wait to get home to find out what this commotion was all about.

We were quickly briefed by the radio announcer: Germany had invaded Poland on September 1, 1939, after peace talks between Hitler and the British Prime Minister Neville Chamberlain had collapsed. England and France had had no choice but to declare war on Germany. They were united once again, their old rivalries put on hold. Their union gave us hope, as well as the confidence we needed to face an uncertain future. The news that the *Wehrmacht* (literally: defense force, German army) had savagely invaded Poland left me feeling sick, powerless, and terribly sad. We saw pictures of the invasion at the movies and in the newsreels.[1] The people of Poland were bombed unmercifully as they left their cities, villages, and hamlets. They were seen leaving on foot, in horse drawn carts, on bicycle, even pushing wheelbarrows loaded with their humble possessions. Before we knew it, the Russians and the Germans had become strong allies, the Russians attacking Poland from the east.

A war had been declared yet no fighting occurred, and even though the allies were at war with Germany, no battles were taking place. There were no fireworks, no display of fighting, and no explosion of bombs. Not only did we feel pretty safe, we also knew that no matter what, the allies were going to be the victors. After all, the French had built the Maginot Line, a line of fortification that was supposedly invincible, along the Siegfried Line, the German line of fortification.[2] We also pinned our hopes on the British air force, the Royal Air Force (RAF). All we had to do was to wait and get ready.

The Belgians, who are practical people, started stocking up on food. My father was the expert on what to purchase. He started to stockpile beans, potatoes, sugar, oil, flour, soap, and all non-perishable staples, which were loaded in a downstairs room. We shared the expert advice of people who had gone through World War I and knew how to keep food from spoiling. The art of canning vegetables and fruit was resurrected, and papa devised ways to make sure that all of the family was involved in canning and making jam and jelly. Yes, we were ready! Still nothing happened except that once in a while a stray plane, either German or British, would fly over the countryside and cause a lot of commotion. The newspapers would chastise whoever was flying aloft. The headlines would sensationalize the event and then return to their same refrain: "NOTHING TO DECLARE ON THE WESTERN FRONT." Life remained somewhat normal, until the beginning of April 1940, when Germany seized Norway and Denmark.

— CHAPTER THREE —

The Nazis Nip at Our Heels

April 9, 1940 remains engraved in my memory. The radio was on when I came home from school at lunchtime, and the announcer declared that Germany had taken Norway and that Denmark would be next. I couldn't believe it. Zap. Zap. Norway—gone. Then Denmark. The tension was mounting, people were on edge and every day the newspapers would repeat the same thing "NOTHING TO DECLARE ON THE WESTERN FRONT." The French referred to that period as *"la drôle de guerre"* or the phony war.

May 10, 1940 marked the end of the phony war. We had expected fireworks but not of the magnitude that followed. The debacle started early in the morning of that balmy day in May. It promised to be a glorious day even at 5:30 in the morning as it was bright daylight already. My sister and I shared a bedroom, my brother had his own; both were located on the fourth floor, or top floor of the house. My parents woke us every morning by ringing a doorbell in our individual rooms. My father controlled the bells from downstairs. My father had come up with the idea because he didn't trust us to respond as rapidly to an alarm clock as we did when they rang that strident, miserable doorbell. My sister and I had planned to go on the yearly school trip that day, but 5:30 AM was too early to be awakened for that event. There was an urgency in the ringing that we couldn't ignore.

Furthermore, we could hear little puff-puff sounds outside in the distance. The clarity of the sky negated the prospect that it was thunder, yet each time we heard the puff sound it was accompanied by white smoke that resembled a tiny cloud. The three of us rushed downstairs where we were met by our parents. We were all concerned when we realized that the puffy sounds and the tiny clouds were anti-aircraft guns. We were being bombed. We were now at war. My sister and I were terribly disappointed, knowing fully well that the school trip was going to be cancelled.

We were glued to the radio listening to our king who exhorted us to be calm and conduct ourselves as great patriots. When they played our national anthem, we rallied and pride swelled our chests. Because Belgium was a small and defenseless country, we felt threatened by Hitler and the Nazis. Yet we felt united and showed a great respect for our king who had had the guts to defy the German army and Hitler. We were now openly on the side of the allies, and we rejoiced at being able to sing without censor all the songs that made fun of the Nazis. Above all we took pride in singing our national anthem, as well as the French *"Marseillaise"* and the British "God Save the King." Even the government controlled radio station started playing songs that made fun of the Siegfied Line, a line of fortifications the Germans had built along the border between Germany and France. We now sang the song openly and gleefully, in both French and English: *"Nous irons pendre notre linge sur la ligne Siegfried"* ("We're gonna hang our wash on the Siegfried Line").

Within a few minutes, the real bombing commenced: heavy bombs started to fall all around us. We had never seen so many planes at once, flying low and letting bombs drop on whatever they might hit. The wailing of the sirens terrified me each time I heard the blast. As directed by the authorities, we took shelter in basements or cellars. We ran for cover to our cellar, not a bad place to stay. The room had been planned as a laundry room, so it had a window and a door opening into a small courtyard and we made it as comfortable as possible. We would trudge upstairs again after the all-clear signal was given and resume our activities. School was closed so time hung heavily on our hands.

On May 11, 1940, there was another commotion in our street. A young man on a motorcycle had stopped in the middle of the street, and his yelling and unruly demeanor attracted the neighbors who listened to what he was saying. He was telling people that he had just come from the Front and had witnessed the power of the German army; he urged us to get out of the city. My father, who was shaving at the time, jumped to the window, raised the sash and started blasting the poor guy, accusing him of being a defeatist, an *agent provocateur* probably paid by the Germans to create a panic. But the young man wouldn't desist. After a few curses directed at my father, he left our street in a puff of black smoke. However, his comments gave food for thought to the young men of the neighborhood. A dozen of them assembled at the Town Hall on their bicycles, but since it was too late to find an army recruiting center and they were all below the recruiting age anyway, they decided to leave Belgium and regroup in France to continue the good fight from the other side of the border. They left Brussels riding their bicycles loaded with possessions packed in saddlebags. My brother eyed them with envy, but my father thought it unreasonable for my brother to follow his friends to an uncertain future. So for the time being my brother reluctantly stayed home.

My father liked to think of himself as a cunning businessman. His independent nature forbade him to work for anybody but himself; therefore, he had developed ways to accomplish the maximum entrepreneurship with a minimum of hard work. He made sure that every house we lived in had an apartment that he could rent out, which would help pay property taxes. That apartment, at 257 *avenue de mai*, was furnished, and papa made sure that the tenants were people of high caliber. It was rented at that time to an Austrian physicist, Joseph Ehrlich, his wife Anna, and their thirteen-year-old daughter, Elizabeth. This Jewish family had escaped Austria and taken refuge in Brussels right after November 9 and 10, 1938, *Kristallnacht,* also called the November Pogrom, the turning point in the Nazi regime of terror. Elie Wiesel calls *Kristallnacht*, "not the beginning but the end of the beginning." That night and the next day, synagogues were destroyed, shops vandalized, a number murdered, and thousands were arrested, and taken to concentration camps. From then on there was no doubt that the Nazis wanted to totally destroy the Jews.

Mr. Ehrlich, a physicist blacklisted by the Nazis because he was Jewish, had earlier been forced to leave the family's native Austria. Now that the Nazis had invaded Belgium, the Ehrlichs were once again in jeopardy and had to try to escape to a more secure country. They left us on May 13, 1940; with incredible luck they took the last boat leaving Ostend, Belgium, for Dover, England. We found out later that they had made it just in time and we were glad to know they had escaped to England. I wish we had done the same.

On May 15, we awoke to rumbling noises again, but this time the noise didn't come from the sky. Part of a British convoy had elected to park its trucks in front of our house, camping there for a few days. We were delighted finally to meet and talk to our allies, real Brits, in uniforms no less. We welcomed them with open arms. We opened our home to them as we had opened our hearts. I finally had the opportunity to try my high school English on them and surprisingly they understood what I was saying. They became the main attraction of our neighborhood, and I was elected translator. Of course, everybody was eager to communicate with our defenders, the British soldiers, first nicknamed "Tommies" during the Boer War. When one of the Tommies asked a friend of mine if he knew English, he replied with honesty, "No, but I can speak French with a British accent."

We, children, would follow the Tommies everywhere they went, trying to anticipate their wishes. Their demeanor inspired trust, they were our hope, and their presence gave us a sense of security. My father let them use the downstairs lavatory (bathroom) and kitchen and left the front door open in order to accommodate their needs. During the day they patrolled with their trucks, walking back and forth with rifles on their shoulders and at the same time walking their mascot, a Jack Russell terrier, on a leash. We cherished these moments and I asked them to sign my diary before they left us. We knew they were going to battle and felt terribly sad when a few days later they actually left us.

After weighing all the imponderables, my father decided that he couldn't face another German occupation. World War I had been enough, so he convinced my mother that the only thing to do was for us to take refuge in France. I hated the idea of leaving my home. All my teenager's dreams came to an abrupt end.

Papa directed the packing of the car. Taking his inspiration from other people who were leaving the neighborhood in droves, he tied a mattress on the roof of the car. He also tied my brother's bicycle to the front of the car. Both the mattress and the bike proved to be lifesavers.

— CHAPTER FOUR —

We Take to the Road

O n May 16, 1940, we pulled out of the driveway. We
locked the door, giving little thought to the memories we
were leaving behind. We were so determined to escape
the Nazis that we were willing to give up our worldly possessions
for the sake of freedom. We dropped our cat at my grandparents'
house, and after effusive and emotional goodbyes, we were on our
way. We piled into papa's old model car; however, my father was
certain that it would take us to our final destination, France,
without trouble.

At this point we were certain that France would remain free
and out of harm's way. My mother's aunt had married a
Frenchman and had settled in the southern part of France a few

years back and their name was going to be given as reference at the border in case we needed a sponsor. To tell the truth my father didn't get along with this uncle and hated the idea of going there, but at least it was reassuring that we had family in France and that we were not totally friendless. I felt secure knowing that we had a destination and were not driving haphazardly to an unknown country. Yet I felt as though I was floating in midair. Everything seemed intangible; decisions were being made for me, and I let the events push me toward a questionable future. At some point I felt paralyzed and unable to speak.

We left Brussels after an early dinner, but just a few miles from our house we encountered bumper-to-bumper traffic. We were barely moving. Then we realized that almost all of Brussels had the same idea—to escape Belgium and the Germans. As we inched our way through the outskirts of Brussels hoping the line of cars would thin out, our hopes were quickly dashed. The line of cars ahead of us was exactly the same as it was in town. We crawled a few feet at a time; then stopped and started again. It was tedious going and our car was a bit recalcitrant, stalling periodically. In addition, it was almost impossible to drive in the dark. We were not allowed to use the headlights, and all the streetlights had been turned off. This was our initiation to the war blackout. So with night upon us and needing gas, papa decided to spend the night on the gas station parking lot. We had no choice but to stay in the car and make the best of it.

We shared that parking lot with several other émigrés who, like us, had decided not to drive at night. We felt secure and rather cozy in the confines of our car as we dozed off to sleep. However, we were awakened after a few minutes by piercing screams and blood curdling sounds coming from a nearby car. The screams couldn't be pacified. The time of night, the lack of a friendly moon, and the darkness gave an eerie feeling to the scene. The blasting siren of an ambulance reinforced the panicky feeling I was experiencing, and searchlights revolving above the ambulance cab added to my discomfort. After a short time and a slamming of several car doors, the night became silent again. Someone told my father that a passenger in a neighboring car had gone mad and had to be taken away. We had been brought up by protective parents, so this was our first contact with such problems. Therefore, this made a lasting impression on us.

Soon we kids were exhausted and fell asleep till morning.

At first light, papa decided to sneak back into the line of cars, which seemed to move a little faster, that is to say we could drive at least five miles without interruption. My father had set his sights on Tournai, a Belgian town close to the French border. It had taken us all that time to travel fifty miles. We were famished by then and papa stopped at a delicatessen where we bought cold cuts to put on crusty French bread. Little did we know that this would be the last French bread we would eat for the next five years. We rinsed the bread down with a glass of our famous Belgian beer, one of the last invigorating beers we would drink.

Papa seemed enthusiastic and upbeat, he loved to be in charge and at that time he seemed to me to be ten feet tall. He gave the impression of being the epitome of self-confidence. I don't think my mother shared my elevated sentiments toward my father. She loved him but not unconditionally, and she was very often heard muttering, "*Mais enfin*, Maurice" (Enough, Maurice), in an exhausted whisper.

We climbed back into the car after a brief inquiry as to the traffic conditions. There were at least five different main roads to the nearest French Frontier post, but we found out that several posts had already been closed because of the influx of refugees. That limited our choice to three, so my father decided to take the second one closest to where we were. As soon as we were out of the town limits we re-encountered the line of cars, as well as hundreds of young men on bicycles and even people walking to freedom. I must admit that there was still a lot of optimism in that array of people. The Belgians were escaping the Nazis in style. There were no horse drawn carts as we had seen in Poland. No, we were driving out of the country. But people were driving away in all sorts of vehicles: funeral hearses had now been equipped to drive the living; even garbage trucks had been refurbished and cleaned in order to accommodate the escapees. Of course there were also brand new cars and the not so brand-new, the sick ones, often demanding a quick fix. The oldest cars, needing extensive repairs, were abandoned on the side of the road. All the vehicles shared one thing: they were crammed with people's precious possessions.

Then my dear papa found a new avocation. He became the savior-of-the-motorist-in-need. As we proceeded in the line of cars, papa would spot the unfortunate responsible for the delay of the moment. He would investigate on foot and try to solve the problem no matter how small or complicated. He would leave us, and because my mother did not drive it meant that we were passed by the cars behind us. Papa would come back to us brimming with sad tales and telling us how he was able to save someone from remaining in Belgium. I believe it was good for his ego.

At one point, we spotted him going in the opposite direction, standing on the running board of a luxury car and giving instruction to the driver. My mother saw him but couldn't believe her eyes. He came back to us a few minutes later explaining that the Countess V had been dropped by her chauffeur. The driver had seen the writing on the wall and had decided right there and then that his skin and his family were as precious as Madame la Contesse's. He had therefore abandoned her in order to save his own flesh and blood. Papa, who had witnessed the treachery of the chauffeur, had come to the rescue, showing the countess how to operate her car, merely giving her driving instructions. As we proceeded due south, my father spotted a huge salami that someone had dropped on the road. "This is a good omen," said my father as he picked it up, adding it to our provisions.

On other occasions, my father was always close at hand to help unfortunate motorists. After leaving the last post my father had spotted a poor soul having trouble starting his engine. This was *the* opportunity my father was seeking to further his higher calling, that is, to follow the Good Samaritan streak he had discovered a few days earlier. Most cars at that time didn't have electric starters and required cranks to start the motors. Apparently there was something wrong with this man's car battery because the poor fellow had trouble managing the steering of the car as well as keeping the car from rolling away from him. My father figured that two people were better than one and at once introduced himself offering to help the stranded motorist. We could see that papa was taking charge of the situation by the way he took the crank from the hands of his new victim and gave orders. When my father was in the process of helping someone, he would bound slightly, and his gait would acquire a certain springy uplifting bounce that made him resemble a bantam rooster. He was in his element. After inquiring as to where he could put the crank (after they had used it unsuccessfully), the poor motorist told my father to put it on the floor behind the driver's seat with "Bomma."

My dad took a look inside the car. Amid a sea of pots and pans, a cage with a canary, blankets, even a small table my father discovered a little old lady squeezed between the window and the array of stuff. You really couldn't stuff another thing in the rear "with Bomma" but that didn't deter the motorist. When looking for a piece of equipment, the answer was the same: "You'll find it in the back seat with Bomma." The poor old lady was incredibly crowded out; she couldn't even sit up straight, yet everything ended up practically on her lap or at her feet. My father was sure that he smelled revenge and that Bomma was not exactly a VIP in that ménage. Madame, the wife, was sitting comfortably in the front seat but was semi-catatonic. We felt sorry for "Bomma," a Brusselese language contraction of *bonne maman* or grandmother. After several unproductive tries with the crank, papa decided as the last resort to push the car down the road hoping to make the motor start by itself. Both he and the motorist put their forces together pushing the car down the incline when suddenly the recalcitrant motor started as by magic, our new friend jumped into his moving vehicle, slammed the door, waved "goodbye" to my father, disappearing in a cloud of smoke and dust.

After the war and even to this day, the back seat of any of our cars is always referred to as Bomma's seat. I never relished being relegated to the Bomma seat when driving with my son-in-law. It didn't take him long to figure out that the Bomma nickname was detestable to me. Guess what my grandchildren call me to this day? They did, however, update Bomma to Bomz.

After this episode, we finally decided to take a road that led us to Mouscron, a small town on the French-Belgian Border. We went through Belgian Customs and showed them the identification they requested. The French controlled the second post. This post was separated from the Belgian post by a short section bordered on both sides by barbed wires, similar to the wires atop a prison wall. That short road we called "No-Man's-Land."

— CHAPTER FIVE —

Almost Across

While we passed through the Belgian checkpoint quickly and without difficulty, afterwards we slowed to a crawl, caught behind a snaking line of cars and people eager to find refuge in France. So, in the middle of No- Man's- Land, we inched forward a few feet at a time. The French let just a few cars go through and when 5:00 PM rolled along, the frontier post closed. It was really pathetic and yet refreshing to realize the French were still behaving as though they were at peace, still sticking to their prewar schedule: the precious 9:00 to 5:00 schedule that had been the object of reform by Leon Blum and his Front Populaire socialist policy during the early thirties. There was nothing to do but wait in line until the next day when the post would reopen.

Because we were tired and hungry my father decided to return to the little town of Mouscron and try the border again the next day early in the morning. We found room at an inn that smelled of stale beer but was otherwise clean. There was only one room available for the five of us, but my resourceful father untied the mattress that we had fastened on the roof of our car and put it on the floor for the three of us to sleep on.

We spent the rest of the day making friends with Dutch people from Amsterdam, escapees like us. We exchanged addresses, promising to see each other again after the allied victory. My father scoured the town, gathering things we might need while waiting for the French to reopen the gates the following day. He was looking mainly for bread, cold cuts, butter, and hard-boiled eggs.

We hit the road early the next morning but once again were detained at the French post. There were many cars ahead of us but we were hopeful; however, most of the time we didn't move at all. Those who waited, as we did, to enter France seemed to be from varied backgrounds. We had been brought up by parents who cherished good manners and despised bad language. The people in the truck in front of us did not pass my parents' stringent standards; to tell the truth those people were rather vulgar and rude. There were three boys, age seven, eight, and nine, I believe, and they relieved themselves right smack in front of us. They had lowered the back gate of the truck, and lining up they peed in unison. I was mortified, and that episode added to my depressed state of mind. I hated to mingle with strangers, and being very class conscious this made a negative impression on me.

The French had panicked at the onslaught of refugees trying to get into their country. They let fewer people enter, but my father was optimistic. We were traveling on a narrow country road where passing was neither permitted nor possible. British convoys that had landed in Cherbourg and Le Havre, France, were going in the opposite direction towards Belgium to fight the war. I know that the refugees hampered their progress. Someone was always trying to break the rule and sneak ahead of the line, which rightly infuriated other drivers. It grew ugly when people tried that little trick.

Yet my father was very understanding and helped some motorist slide ahead of us providing the case he presented was viable. However to make it sound reasonable to the cars around us papa would raise his voice, brandish the salami we had picked up from the road all the while whispering under his breath to the sneaker to "go ahead" and not tell the others that he was letting him go. I remember him telling a very nice gentleman that if he dared pass in front of us he would slash his tires and make neckties out of them all the while motioning him to go ahead. His screams and threats pacified the motorists around us who sided with my father while the culprit raced down the road as quickly as he could get away. Papa even let another car sneak between us and the truck with its load of vulgar kids. Was he really that altruistic? I believe he did that in order to block our view of the truck and its vulgar human content.

At 5:00 PM the French closed the gates again. But this time we stayed put, determined to spend the night in our car. Nobody moved. The crowd was silent. And so were we. Before leaving home my father had the brilliant idea of tying my brother's bike to the front of the car, a decision that proved so valuable as to be near genius. My restless brother rode his bike up and down the line of cars and started the countdown. He found out there were 364 cars ahead of us. My father thought it was a good number and once again was optimistic but to me the number appeared astronomical. I envied my father's optimism as I retreated more into myself regretting the loss of my home, which all of a sudden became heaven.

— CHAPTER SIX —

Attacked

The next day was sunny and warm. We thanked God for weather so favorable. Right before dusk some people decided to spend the night in the fields away from their parked cars. We had seen them filing out carrying their blankets, preparing to sleep *a la belle etoile* (under the clear star studded sky). They behaved as though they were going on a camping vacation. Some of them had rolled sleeping bags and were making friends with their fellow travelers. The mood of that throng of people was jovial; they were certainly making the whole thing enviable to us kids. We approached papa with the idea that we could do the same and at least to let us kids "have some fun." Papa nixed that prospect on the spot, invoking fundamentals of good manners, etiquette, devotion, and respect to parents. "No!" and that was that.

A little later we heard a purring sound right above our heads. It was not loud but it was steady, then the purring noise increased and made us look in all directions. Suddenly, we spotted a German fighter plane diving over us and we heard the "tac-tac-tac" noise of a machine gun exploding right over us, hitting both the line of refugees and those who had chosen to sleep in the fields. Panic seized the crowd as people ran helter-skelter, screaming and howling in every direction.

The fighter plane turned around and once again flew over us strafing the innocent refugees. That plane was so close we could almost have touched it. Then after having done its dirty deed it flew away leaving us horrified. The little community we had created remained transfixed with fear.

In the fields just a few feet away the moaning of the wounded made us both fearful and sick. Few dared walk out to help the wounded. Yet some courageous men, who had elected to stay in their cars, as we had done, went to the rescue of the wounded. We were shaking with fear but our fright was so intense that we couldn't even cry. My parents did their best to hide the horrible spectacle from us. My brother was at once dispatched to a nearby farm to ask for help. He climbed on his bike and sped down the road hoping to find a farm with a phone to call for an ambulance.

Divine Providence had again made us stay inside the car, but papa rectified our thinking and told us in no uncertain terms that we had been protected by remaining in our car under the mattress that was tied to its roof. Now we heard the screeching of the sirens in the distance, and an ambulance came to the aid of the victims. We were more full of hate than scared, our pent up rage surged at what the Nazis had done. The attack made us want to scream and deny the existence of God. Yet we remained silent; deep hatred made us speechless. What the Nazis had done was proof of their lack of humanity, and this last foray reinforced our hatred of our enemy.

— CHAPTER SEVEN —

Still Seeking Safety

All five of us slept crunched up in the car. European cars of that day were not plush—certainly not as wide as their American counterparts. The next day my brother went to the farm again but this time to get milk and water and, of course, to gather some information about the previous night's events. Since my brother was "mobile" he became the pet of the people in line. The refugees asked him to bring provisions the farmers could spare and he was proud to oblige. The farmers, on the other hand, quickly realized the value of the law of supply and demand; their water became liquid gold, their bread, ingots; and they started to gouge the poor people. My father watched but said nothing. He simply took my brother's bike and rode to the nearby farm and very nicely asked the farmer to state how much he charged for a bottle of water and a loaf of bread. The farmer named an exorbitant price. Papa shook a box of matches vigorously like tiny castanets while eyeing a stack of very flammable hay and asking the farmer once more to state his prices. There were no threats on the part of my father; however, the noise of the rattling matches in the little box and the firm tone of my father's voice made the trembling farmer reduce his prices drastically. I bet he could visualize the fireworks his haystacks could produce.

Another night came and, once again we were obliged to spend it in the line to the French Post. We had made friends with people around us, exchanging bits of news we had heard on the radio. It didn't sound good: the Germans bombing towns around us and even talk of Nazi advances and gains of territory. The amateur strategists were in their element remembering what had happened during World War I; they were certain that this was just a little setback for the allies. When night came I watched the sky turn from a bright glorious blue to a flaming, bloody red. Yet the red was not static, but seemed to be shimmering on the horizon. We were rather intrigued by the eerie spectacle, wondering what was making the sky so red. We discovered that Abbeville, France, was being bombed unmercifully, and the flames consuming that city could be seen from our car.

At dusk there was a slight commotion. Two men going from car to car were asking everyone to remain silent for a while. They explained that some one had died in the line and a few minutes later we saw two strapping men who had been elected pallbearers carrying a body stretched on a ladder. They carried the ladder over their heads as they passed silently by us. The whole scenario is still vivid in my mind—the dreadful spectacle silhouetted against the flames of the burning city. It was eerie and upsetting. We didn't want to look at that makeshift funeral cortege out of respect for the dead person but I sneaked a peek and my sadness was renewed. He was an elderly man who had died abruptly, we assumed, from natural causes, for reasons unrelated to the war.

This reinforced the idea that, despite the war, life as well as death from natural causes go on—at least from my fifteen-year-old perspective.

Our brief stay in this "No- Man's- Land" was striking to me for many reasons, not least of which was the absolute lack of privacy. On a public road there are no bathrooms, no showers, no sinks, and no toilets. Inside the car I felt trapped but afraid to leave it for fear that the column of cars would forge ahead and, even worse, that my parents would forget me. The whole commotion upset my system and I started having my period at that inconvenient time and place. I felt diminished and the fact that we had chosen to be uprooted dawned on me for the very first time. That thought must have been overpowering to me because I can't to this day remember having hunger pains during the "trip." I don't remember what our conversations were about or what my brother and sister were thinking. I was wrapped in my own sorry state of affairs and ignored everyone around me. I don't even remember if we quarreled.

The next day the French closed their borders. Our choices were few: we could either turn back and go either home or to our summer house, or we could hope that the French would reconsider and let us in. They didn't change their minds.

We tried to enter France at several other frontier posts, but the roads were still encumbered by hundreds of cars hoping to escape the Nazis. We then decided that because we were so close to the sea, we ought to go to our summerhouse. The town of Blankenberg was the last garrison of the Belgian army. Belgian soldiers had been hurriedly called to serve the country and were not exactly dressed for battle. They wore their uniforms, but several wore wooden shoes, and some of them even had the slippers they were wearing when the call came. The troops were ill prepared both in machines and outlook; they were fighting tanks and sophisticated weaponry on horseback. The only thing they wanted to do was "to save their skin," as they explained to my father when he accused them of being cowards for not continuing to fight. They would shake their fists in my father's face as a way to justify their act of cowardice. It was rather pathetic to witness a defeated army, folding under enemy superiority. My father was appalled.

Moreover, the news on the radio was terrible. The throng of refugees on the road from Belgium to France had impeded the progress of the British army who had trouble reaching the battlefield. Our king, Leopold III, wavering, lacked the courage to exhort his men to continue fighting for freedom. On the other hand, how could an army whose soldiers wore wooden shoes and rode on horseback face the highly polished and refined war machine of the Nazis? We were asked by the local authorities not to step on the beach but to stay home. (The beach may have been mined or perhaps they suspected an attack from the sea.) The sirens blasted constantly and we were bombed unmercifully.

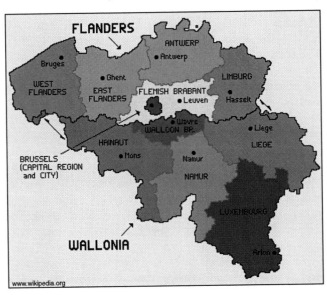

www.wikipedia.org

— CHAPTER EIGHT —

The King Surrenders

Then on May 28, 1940, our king, Leopold III surrendered, choosing to stay in Belgium. As far as I was concerned this was treason. I could not accept this. I felt as though my world was crumbling around me. Once again I became very depressed and really hated Leopold for his cowardice. His cabinet chose to flee to England to continue the fight and support the Allied cause. We thought: what a blow to the memory of King Albert I, the courageous man who stood up to the Kaiser. And what were we left with? My father raged, bluntly declaring, "At chess a king never surrenders." However, this was not chess; this was real war, and we had all hoped that our king would follow his cabinet and choose freedom in England.[3]

When news from the capital started to filter down, people in the streets could not understand the king's decision. Brussels had fallen to the Germans even though the Belgian army had blown up the bridges straddling the canal and a mere rivulet that divides Brussels in two unequal parts. These measures had been used during the First World War in order to slow the progress of the Kaiser's army but they proved inadequate against a German military machine so potent that it was redefining warfare. The king had betrayed us, and for my family this was time to make a decision to return to Brussels. We repacked the car and headed down to Brussels one hundred kilometers down the road.

We now left our summer shore home and began to cross the flat country known as the Flanders, made famous in a John McCrae poem "In Flanders Field," and known for the decisive battle there in 1918, during World War I.[4] The Flanders are lovely, flat but green, that liquid green of countries like Ireland that receive their fair share of rain. You can smell grass and dew, and even the sun that filters through the northern light has a smell. The roads were bordered by poplars, tall and thin, standing at attention and evenly spaced, as though inspired by Monet.

Yet in the midst of all this beauty was carnage so great that I wanted to vomit. Our soldiers had surrendered their weapons and piles of rifles lined the road. The horses they had ridden against the Panzer Divisions were lying dead, their bellies distended, their legs sticking up in the air. Some soldiers were gathered in vacant lots waiting to be transported to prison in Germany, while others were walking in small groups stone-faced, dejected, and ashamed.

We hadn't seen a German soldier, although we were about twenty-five miles from Brussels. No need to tell you that we were not in a hurry to meet the dreaded enemy.

— CHAPTER NINE —

Culture Shock!

Then, we saw them—*Les Boches*, the Germans. At first I shaded my eyes and avoided looking at them. However, curiosity got the best of me and I peeked. There they were, looking cool and walking down our boulevards as though they had been born there. They walked on, hardly paying attention to us. They infuriated me—to see their demeanor, that they seemed to be at home in my town, in my country. Their uniforms didn't impress me at all; indeed, the officers' uniforms made me crack up. Papa was also laughing openly and telling to all who could hear: "If ridicule were lethal, those Krauts would be dead."[5] The officers' hats were ostentatious and too theatrical for my taste. Their uniforms were trimmed in silver, loads of it; to me they looked more like Hollywood operetta characters than military men.

We arrived home and had trouble opening the front door. Bombs, dropped while we were on the road trying to escape, had put the house out of kilter and the door was jammed. After we opened it, it was difficult to close it again so we lived with a door ajar for years to come. The house was intact; nothing was missing, nobody had come in.

We rushed to the corner grocery store to buy some needed supplies but found the store practically empty. The shelves had been emptied by the people who had remained in Brussels and because of the fighting, we presumed, the shelves had not been restocked. We hoped that since the fighting had stopped, normalcy would resume and that some supplies would be forth coming. But this was not to be. My mother wanted to buy some bread, but the shopkeeper told her that in order to buy it she had to present a coupon that was available at city hall. And believe me, there were no exceptions—no ticket, no bread. My father was reminiscing about his First World War tribulations. "See, they haven't changed."

The next day my parents went to the Borough Hall with our identification cards and received a sheet of stamps of different colors. Each member of the family received the same sheet, with the same number of coupons or rather stamps. One sheet had to last one month of thirty days. There were thirty stamps for bread. Thirty for meat, four for butter, one for sugar, and thirty for milk. However, we needed five stamps to get one loaf of bread, which weighed about one pound. Try to feed a family of five, three of them, teenagers, on these rations, and you have famine nipping at your stomach. Meat was something else. For one pound of beef or pork, we had to surrender twenty stamps, which meant that we ate meat only once a week generally on Sunday. We had to discover other ways to get protein. Flour was unavailable; coffee, non-existent. We were forced to drink some awful brew made of roasted oat kernels mixed with bitter chicory to give it flavor. The word *flavor* is far fetched. Butter was replaced by margarine, and even at that, we had to make do with a stick of margarine a week. Milk was skimmed, and potatoes also were cruelly regulated. One kilo a week. Maybe. Belgians are potato eaters but so are the Germans; therefore, our potato production was shipped immediately to the German troops stationed in Germany or in Belgium, France, and Holland.

A trip to the department stores told another sad tale. No clothes, no shoes, no stockings. The German women had been snooping around our well-appointed stores and had bought everything they could put their hands on. For years those poor women had been restricted and had to make do with very little. Many had never worn silk stockings and the German fashions were not comparable to French elegance, so they had a blast. These women were in the German army, which was a revelation to us. We had never seen military women. They wore gray uniforms, which we described as being the color of *gris souris effrayee*, which means "frightened mouse" gray. They were not carrying weapons, so they looked all right, I thought. We girls would look them over, that's the nature of the beast, yet they struck me as being healthy and strong looking. We used to browse in the department stores hoping that something would be available but nothing ever was. Yet the German women always bought things that we couldn't buy. We lacked the coupons; they had them. At the sight of those fighting women, my brother would become crazy. After spotting one he would run in her immediate vicinity and ambush her so to speak. He would stick his foot out from behind a counter and trip the German woman, who yelled loudly while falling. It was fun for us because we knew where to find Guy by the yell of the *fraulein*. This pinpointed my brother's position without trouble.

If we wanted to eat meat, we had to grow our own, so to speak. Papa decided to raise our own poultry starting from chicks to chicken. Unfortunately, *How to Raise Chickens for Dummies* hadn't been written, so we gathered a lot of information from farmers who did not always welcome our inquiries. We were lucky to find chicks that promised to grow into hens. The hens could lay eggs, a great source of protein, and in turn the hens would eventually end up in the pot.

There was also the idea of raising rabbits. Belgians are fond of this very tender meat and my father built hutches the best way he could. After all papa was an engineer and nothing was a secret to him. He built four hutches for the bunnies. It was not easy to feed the rabbits, but we managed. My mother boiled potato peels mixed with any greens we could find and they chewed their fodder happily, silently, seriously. Rabbits are serious animals and incredibly cute, so to regard these pets as a meal in the making was very hard on us. The hardest part of all was incumbent to my father who had chosen to kill the rabbits upon their maturity. Papa couldn't do it, he had to enlist the help of a farmer to do it for him and I remember wearing a black armband to school the day after an opulent repast as a form of respect for our fallen bunny. We were in deep mourning. We even tanned the skins.

The rabbits were fertile and the chicks were growing, but not without a few catastrophic problems. Some of the chicks that had been sold to us as hens turned out to be roosters, and some of them were in bad shape. They had diarrhea, a common ailment in baby chicks. My brother was not only concerned about their bad health but had vowed to save the brood. He gave the baby chicks some concoction of thyme oil that had to be sneaked into their tiny beaks with an eyedropper. My brother was very patient and every day he would flip the chicks on their backs and flex their little legs in rhythm. He was not only patient as I mentioned above but he took his job as chick savior very seriously. He would come upstairs late for dinner and reply to our mother's inquisitions that he had been doing gymnastics with the baby chicks. It was very tedious work and sometimes his efforts were for naught. And despite his effort some of them died but the survivors rewarded him a few weeks later by laying their first eggs. I want to add that we *never* ate the hens we had raised. As for the roosters they used to scare my mother to death. They would spy on her, look for a moment of inattention in order to chase her round and round the small courtyard, and then jump violently, hitting her with their talons and beaks. Those roosters' tough carcasses ended in the pot without the benefit of a weeping eulogy.

— CHAPTER TEN —
Life Under Nazi Rule

Life went on, and after we had settled to a routine we made contact with our friends to compare notes and commiserate. We were very surprised to find that some of our friends were rather impressed by the Nazis. The soldiers of the Third Reich were not the same as the Kaiser's soldiers, they said. They did not commit the atrocities the Kaiser's armies did in 1914. They minded their business and left us alone. And that in itself threw the WW I veterans for a loop. They had expected violence on the part of the occupying forces. Even my grandfather, seeing an approaching soldier, stepped into the gutter and gave the soldier room on the sidewalk, marveling at the fact that the soldier hadn't slapped him, an incident that had happened during the other war.

Since school was still in session, we resumed our studies, but the atmosphere there was strange. Nobody expressed their feelings openly. If you were too anti- Nazi, people gave you the cold shoulder. I could not figure out what was going on until one friend told me confidentially that my opinions were not to be aired nor discussed.

We quickly found out that it was the Gestapo who did the dirty job and not openly either. Any citizen had the right to turn you in to the Gestapo if you were heard criticizing the regime, and in many cases it was the Gestapo who put you into prison without the benefit of a hearing or a trial.

It didn't take long for the people who had been impressed earlier by the power of the Nazis to quickly change their minds. Papa was not duped by their behavior. A few weeks after the Belgian surrender, all males over thirty years of age received a questionnaire from the Nazis asking them to state their skills, health status, profession and other facts that could help the Nazis select some strong and healthy men for the armament factories in Germany. Papa could smell a rat and wrote across the paper, "I shall resume my pre-war activities after the Allied Victory." The Nazis could have viewed this as treasonous and upon reflection it could be thought of as carelessness on my father's part because he was putting his entire family in jeopardy. But we thought it was the right thing to do and congratulated my father on his heroism.

Life became more and more arduous in many ways. We were reduced to doing with very little food and to watching for "specials": a shipment of potatoes or sugar that was available at certain stores. My patient sister was the best one to queue up and stay somewhere in line for hours to get an extra pound of potatoes or a kilo of sugar. In fact, she lined up any time she saw a line of people waiting in front of a store, totally unaware of what was being offered, just in case it could be some staple we needed. My brother Guy proudly came home with his find, some rabbit pâté guaranteed not to contain rabbit, but the ad on the can was phrased so cleverly that it could have fooled any teenager.

When school started again in September, the kids who had tried to leave the country with their parents, came back to resume life as usual and with stories to tell. We learned that a Spanish classmate of mine along with her family, on her way back to Spain, had been machine-gunned by the Nazis in a trench on the side of a road. This struck me because this was the first time I had lost a friend my age.

My best friend, Angele, became very elusive and terribly mysterious to me. She didn't share her thoughts with me, which intrigued me. Teenage girls are known to be chatty, but Angele became silent—an impenetrable silence. She had a brother, Marcel, who was maybe three years older than she. He was an Eagle Scout and was always around young men his age. They talked of things that didn't interest me and I quickly found out that I was not interesting to them. To me, however, they were hunks, very virile, and some of them even smoked pipes. Their tobacco was revolting. I used to visit my friend quite often just to look at Marcel and also at one of his friends, who was particularly fascinating—and not because he had one brown eye and a blue one, but because he was charming. His brother was also an Eagle Scout, but he was Angele's boyfriend. Their mother was French and both young men took after mama, speaking French flawlessly which added to their attractiveness. Angele was a musician and played the piano like an angel, which made it fun for us despite the gloomy mood of the prevailing war tensions. We had sing-alongs you wouldn't believe. The father, a *fonctionnaire*, a state employee, was related to farmers in the countryside very close to Brussels.

At that time it became essential to know someone "in the country," a farmer who could sell you some unattainable staple. Angele and her family always welcomed my sister and me and invited us for dinner, knowing that my parents didn't know anybody "in the country," that we lacked the extra things that could have made life more agreeable. They had bacon and white flour, and Angele's mother made some great bread. All in all those people were very nice to my sister and me and we became very good friends.

One of the most important things to do was collect recipes on how to make something out of nothing. The Belgians had WW I experience and started trading recipes they had had in the past. We made bread by mixing flour with mashed potatoes, in order to save flour and give body to the bread. Result: some heavy and hard-to-digest concoction.

One day my father came home with a bag of oat kernels that had fallen from a cart pulled by horses. I assumed these were for the horses; however, my parents thought we could eat the oats. We immediately started to grind the barbed kernels and tried to sift the resulting flour the best we could. Yet it was difficult to separate the bran from the flour and its texture was incredibly coarse. We found out that the husks of the kernel were like straw. But my mother made a cake from that rough flour anyway and to add insult to injury she put too much baking soda, guessing the flour would have a hard time to rise by itself. Therefore, the end product was so coarse that it became clear we could not eat it and the strong taste of the baking soda made it even more revolting. There were spikes that hurt the inside of our mouths. Even to my brother—who ate everything—this concoction was inedible. He remarked wisely, "If you think that stuff hurts going in, you can imagine what it does on its way out." Not to worry, my brother's friend Pelot found it delicious and ate it with gusto. Needless to say, Pelot was hungrier than we and showing it. He was terribly skinny. He had lost the cap of his front tooth; only the gold plate that held the porcelain showed and collected particles of food. To look at him was therapeutic in a way. You didn't feel hungry for a few hours.

Pelot came from a very large family, very bohemian, very intellectual, yet at first the family was quite impressed by the Nazis. Madame deBoignie, Pelot's mother, raved about the chivalry of the *new* German army and how one day, so she told us—acting on her own—she had stopped a convoy of heavily loaded trucks by just waving her hand, and upon spotting her the line of trucks came to a screeching halt and let her cross the avenue at her own pace. Big deal! She could not believe the Nazis' chivalry. However, being intelligent had its rewards; it didn't take long for those people (including Madame de B) to change their minds and realize that the Nazis were indeed our enemy. Still we were quite reluctant to air our views in front of them for fear of being denounced to the Gestapo.

We never knew about people for sure. Once they had praised the Nazis it became hard for us to trust them implicitly. After all, we loved our freedom even though it was controlled. I knew about Angele, my enigmatic buddy. I knew I could trust her and her family. But Pelot? He belonged to a Catholic youth organization headed by a young priest, Father Florizoon, who was anti–Nazi. However, the Vicar, Father Deknoop, was more reluctant to state his views openly. It was fun to go to mass on Sunday and guess what he actually meant when he made innuendoes that had undertones of anti-Nazism. We were delighted to see that most of our friends were coming around and rallying to the sacred cause of our allies. Although Father Deknoop was anti-Nazi, he respected King Leopold III and remained enigmatic as far as his personal thoughts about the king were concerned. After all Leopold was a king by divine right, come to think of it, and I suppose that was the rationale behind Father Deknoop's reluctance to brand our treacherous king.

— CHAPTER ELEVEN —

Revenge of the Teenagers

L ife continued for us kids with a semblance of normalcy. We returned to school but we found out that teenagers had no value to the Nazis. We were too young, too small, and too immature to be an asset to the party. But, oh how we did bug them. The soldiers used to wear some unbecoming, ridiculous-looking raincoats. These raincoats were made of imitation rubber, the forerunner of plastic, and we rapidly found out that they were incredibly flammable.

We would welcome a poor *Wehrmacht* soldier on a crowded streetcar platform by sneakily putting a lighted cigarette by his raincoat that would immediately burst into flames. After a few episodes, people were forbidden to smoke on the streetcar platform, but that didn't curtail our devilry. Instead of lighted cigarettes, we used acid that students lifted from the school labs. No, there were no flames but the acrid smell that emanated from the eaten ersatz-rubber was awful.

That was the beginning of our harassment of our oppressors.

As the war progressed, there was more and more harassment. One branch of the German army was particularly disgusting to us: the *National Sozialisches Kraftfahr Korps* (the NSKK).[6] Basically they were drivers who had been elevated to almost saintly status ánd had one advantage. They could understand French. Many mistakenly thought the Nazis did not regard this group with high esteem, and many mistook them for just another branch of the party. However, the NSKK were zealots and more deeply indoctrinated to Nazism than many other branches of the military. They were ready to fight us kids at the drop of a hat and because they could understand French to a certain extent, we had to be careful choosing our insults. At the sight of one of them my favorite trick was to swing my schoolbag erratically and aim it where it really hurt. This would always be followed by a piercing yell, a grabbing of the crotch, vociferous swearing and generally a slap in the face of the attacker. I remember receiving one slap, given with such violence that it put my jaw out of commission for years to come. I guess I had muttered "*sale cochon*," dirty pig, which he had alas understood and even when I tried to find a homonym for "*cochon*" in order to diffuse the impact of the insult, he gave me the slap with his fist. I wore my injury with glory.

One time, in 1941, when Peter II (*Pierre deux* in French), prince regent of Yugoslavia, became a victim of Hitler, he was regarded as a hero by the oppressed Belgians. We heard through the grapevine that he had been betrayed to the Axis Nations. After the invasion of his country the unfortunate prince had to flee to Greece for a while. We remembered that the area of a circle's formula was "Pi-R-squared" or PI-R-2 (πR^2) pronounced in French as *PIERRE DEUX*. In a very short time kids scribbled the formula on every wall space available honoring the prince in a subtle way by those clever Belgians. It was our small contribution to another war hero.

Of course, since we had no value to the Nazis, we became very useful to the underground. We were a negligible quantity to the Nazis but because of our transparency to them, we became invaluable to the *maquis*, the famous Belgian-French underground entity.[6] As I learned later in the war, my friend Angele's brother and his friends were all part of that underground organization, and I believe that this was the reason for their total ignorance of my sister's and my existence. They were busy with more important responsibilities. My brother, fifteen years old at the onset of the war, was anxiously waiting to do something important for the resistance effort. He was perfect for the part he would later play.

— CHAPTER TWELVE —

Underground Activities

My father became more and more patriotic as the days went by and the bad news from the front didn't deter his faith in the Allied victory. He knew for certain that they were going to win the war, despite losing these battles. The low morale and pessimism of his peers prompted him to publish an underground newsletter. It was no easy task to print something when printing supplies were at a premium. At the onset of the occupation my father had to find some steady employment since he refused to work as an engineer, which could have been useful to the Nazis. He found a temporary job with a savings bank that became the supplier of the paper, ink, stencils, and other materials he desperately needed. He named his paper *La Belgique Opprimee,* which means *The Oppressed Belgium,* relishing the hours spent venting the clandestine feelings he harbored for the enemy. My brother became his "mule," distributing the newsletter to his schoolmates.

It became increasingly difficult to listen to the BBC. The Germans had a way of interfering with the airwaves, scrambling the signals, and at news time it was hard to listen to the news, which was always depressing. My father felt that he had an obligation to listen to the BBC in order to inform his readers. Yet it was forbidden to listen to any news about the allies, so he didn't want to be caught. This would have landed him in jail. However, sometimes the bulletins were clear as a bell and we became acquainted with the French announcers whom we loved from afar.

I still remember their names: Pierre Bourdan and Jean Marin. They were strong in their exhortations to be courageous, not to give up, thus reviving our faltering faith and sagging spirits. They started their commentaries with vigor and their voices denoted strength when they announced "*Honneur et Patrie voici la France Libre*," which translated "Honor and Country, listen to Free France."

The news bulletins were always interrupted midstream by "personal messages," phrases that had little meaning to us, but we were fascinated by them. The messages could be something as mundane as "the dog is playing in the street," given at the same time every day and would be broadcasted until the message was received by the interested party, so sometimes the message would be repeated every day for a week, a month or sometimes only a day.

Papa's newsletter became very important to all of us. It revived my father's will so he could take his loss of freedom with grace without being violent. Our greatest loss was our loss of the freedom we held so dear, the inability to speak out, to be careful of every word we uttered for fear of being put in jail without benefit of a trial. The fact that we were forced to be silent and face the terrible injustices we witnessed made us feel as though we were accomplices to a regime we despised.

We were proud of my father for expressing his feelings, and his patriotism made us love our country fiercely. Patriotism was in full swing, which is a switch, usually teenagers are too cool to be patriotic, but now it became like a burning flame inside of us.

However, we were forbidden to sing our national anthem either at school or at other events. My sister, Ginette, went to a different school from mine, and her principal was a woman of great strength, Mademoiselle Lemaire. She was not afraid to assemble the whole school in the auditorium, asking the children to sing the national anthem silently. She used to do this every once in a while especially when the going was rough. My sister knew that they all sang silently by the fierce look in some kids' eyes, the quivering lips of others, and the goose pimples she experienced herself. Thank God, that wonderful woman was never denounced to the Gestapo.

— CHAPTER THIRTEEN —

Subversive Activities

O ur house was a four-story building, not including the cellars. On the ground floor were the garage, my father's office, a kitchen, a toilet, and the door to the cellars, with all the doors opening on a long hallway. A flight of stairs took us to our apartment, which included the kitchen, the dining room, the living room, my parents' bedroom, and the bathroom. Another flight of stairs led to the next floor, which was a duplicate of our living quarters. My father rented out that apartment.

Another flight of stairs took us to the top floor where our quarters, the kids', were located. Next to our room was a guest room, and next to that was the attic. The attic was unfinished but we could get under the roof by climbing a ladder, which gave access to the forbidden region of our house. (We were forbidden to be up there; my parents considered it dangerous.) There was a skylight in the roof and another skylight opening to the guest room. This was an indoor skylight that my father had dubbed "the architect's mistake." It let just a little light enter the guest room, but it didn't really open.

Our house was located on the outskirts of Brussels, in a new area being built one street at a time, where all houses were inhabited by their owners instead of renters, and each house differed in size and architecture. It was not a development. Most of our neighbors were from the middle class, well educated; many were business people but not with large fortunes. Although they were close to each other, each house had a very small garden leading to the house entrance, and many of our neighbors—we didn't—had a garden in the back. We had a paved courtyard on the same level as the cellar and surrounded by brick walls eight feet high capped with shiny tiles. That wall was very difficult to scale, but I had mastered its scaling.

Mr. Ehrlich, the Austrian physicist, his wife, and daughter, who had rented the apartment above ours before the war had fled

Austria because of the Nazis' persecution of the Jews; therefore, the family obviously could not stay in Brussels under the Nazi occupation. They left Belgium on May 11,1940, just a day after the invasion. The apartment was empty; however, my father refused to declare it vacant for fear of having it requisitioned by the Nazis, but our neighbor across the street pointed it out to some German soldiers who were inquiring about lodgings and then my father had no other choice.

The apartment was immediately rented by a German family, consisting of a man, his wife, and a little girl, Gretchen. They were civilians. I can't remember the names of the father or the mother except that their last name was Heumann. We were never on first name basis anyway. This was not done in Europe; people are more formal there. Madame Heumann was a tall blond, and what my sister admired most were her hands. They were well proportioned, but Ginette was fascinated by her nails, which for my sister was natural since she herself possessed the longest set of nails, always properly manicured and very shiny. Madame H's nails were big and well shaped. Mr. Heumann was a tall, heavy-set man, the stereotype of the Germans we used to see in the comics. He was too young to have a fold of fat in the nape of his neck, but I am sure he was prone to it. I nicknamed him "the sack." At first we were friendly toward one another but we avoided talking politics. The husband used to sell razor blades and scales before the war, but we didn't know what he was now doing in Belgium as a civilian.

Madame Heumann, who was born in Hamburg, was young, very athletic, and a first rate swimmer. She used to tell us that she swam in the Kiel Canal and used tin cans for floaters. She loved to knit and used to do so in rhythm with German marching music that gave us the creeps. She also held her knitting needles differently from us, holding the needles the way you hold a pencil when you write. We hold our needles under the arms. Boy . . . she was forceful, one-two-one-two, *ein-zwei-ein-zwei* . . . click clack went the needles. Madame Heumann was also pregnant.

With the Heumanns in the house, we had to be more careful about everything. My father's newsletter had to be printed more secretly than ever before. Papa also started writing a book about the German mentality and their hereditary hunger for war. He used to call it his "Masterpiece," but if he had been found writing it, he would have landed in jail.

The Heumanns had the terrible habit of bursting into our quarters without knocking, which made life more perilous for us. They would simply open the door, then knock, and take a bird's eye view of what was happening in our home. There were some panicky moments, especially since they both spoke French fluently. Papa even suggested putting thumbtacks in front of our door, on the doormat to make the intruder scream before bursting into our apartment. I don't know why we never did this.

My father guessed that Mr. H. must have been spying for the Nazis in Belgium before the war. The Heumanns used to entertain and care for Hans, a soldier from the *Wehrmacht*, who used to come and visit at least once a week. It was frightening to encounter an enemy soldier in the hallway and hear the clunking of his hobnailed boots on the wooden stairs, but he was always polite and tried to converse with us kids. He also used to knock on our door, leave a loaf of bread on the doorstep or downstairs on the hallway radiator, and vanish before we could thank him. Nobody knew about it but us. Hans was a decent man.

Now the Germans started to assail us with propaganda posters glued all over building walls in Brussels. These posters had disgusting messages as well as disgusting pictures. My sister, brother, and I ripped them off before the glue had time to set. One of Mr. Roosevelt sitting on a toilet was especially vulgar and obnoxious to us. The caption was about "Invasion Oil!" and mocked him because he had not invaded yet. The Germans were trying to goad Roosevelt—although they would have been afraid if the United States had invaded. Moreover, the Germans were trying to poison our minds about Roosevelt whom we revered and adored. While we were having a great time ripping the poster, Mrs. Heumann had been looking at us from the other side of the street and telling us that we were naughty children. Since she was pushing a baby carriage, she was unable to run after us. Somehow she put the incident out of her head and considered it more of a teenage prank than an insult to the Third Reich.

Although they were Nazis in good standing, the Heumanns didn't fare too well as far as food was concerned. Their government provided the food, which they could get without coupons, and it was more plentiful than what we could buy. They were allowed potatoes and dried beans in great quantity; they had butter, which we didn't, but instead of honey they had some fake sugar that was sweet, syrupy, very fluid and pearly white. They also had cocoa powder strangely enough and coffee. They used to store their potatoes in the cellar and used the dumbwaiter to store their perishables.[8] The dumbwaiter's purpose was to haul coal from the cellar to our apartment, but because we didn't have coal anyway, it became obsolete for that purpose, so the Heumans used it as a refrigerator, keeping it loaded with their food and sending the dumbwaiter all the way down, in the cool cellar.

The temptation was tremendous for us. There was food in their cellar, available to us because we had the duplicate key. How easy it was to help ourselves to their food. But in moderation. Ginette, my sister, was great at stealing. My brother Guy used to steal the pseudo honey and mix it in a small bowl with the cocoa powder and share the mess with us . . . Yukkk. I also tried my hand at pilfering but was so nervous about the crime that the following Sunday I confessed it to our vicar Father De Knoop. I was terrified to tell the good priest of my sin but my father was inflexible and told me in no uncertain term to go confess. I was crying loudly and the congregation was rather perturbed by my display of guilt. I stumbled into the confessional and told the good priest—after having mumbled the act of contrition—that I had stolen food.

"Why did you steal it? Were you hungry?" he asked me, putting words into my mouth.

"Yes, Father," was my answer. "Whom did you steal it from?" At that point I felt sure that he knew the answer. "I stole from the Germans who live upstairs, Father," I whispered. "Go in peace my child, stealing from the enemy is no sin. You have to survive; therefore, you are forgiven," he replied without hesitation, "but for good measure just say one or two 'Our Fathers' and one 'Hail Mary.'" He gave me his blessing and I left the church a relieved sinner with the promise to myself not

to do it again. At that precise moment I knew that Father
Deknoop was a patriot, a friend.

*On the negative side many sins were now condoned by our
parents as well as by la sainte eglise; stealing from the enemy was
not only justified, but encouraged. Lying and cheating became
part every day life and practiced casually in the name of self-
defense. Killing was pardoned providing it resulted in the
extermination of a foe. The values we held so dearly before the war
were now crushed. But in the end, our will and determination
combined with our faith in the victory of the allies prevailed. After
the war we reverted to our former values—lying, stealing, cheating,
and killing were again sins.*

However, when I rejoined my father after that confession, papa
told me in no uncertain terms that a young lady going to
confession should always keep her cool and should NEVER enter
the privacy of the confessional with tears streaming down her face.
The "think about what the neighbors are going to think about
when they see you in such a state" came up; then I realized that
girls going to confession have a moral obligation to remain non-
committal and show no emotion. My father was certain that the
parishioners were going to brand me as a girl of loose morals,
facing an illegitimate pregnancy.

We had another friend, a retired army chaplain who lived with
his sister. He used to walk his German shepherd on a leash every
day. That man for sure was openly anti-Nazi and wasn't afraid to
advertise his patriotism. He was a good friend of the lady who
owned a pastry shop, Madame Fourneau, who, alas, didn't sell
pastry anymore; instead she sold that terrible bread we had to eat
every day. He revived our spirits also by talking in a loud voice in
the street, as some kind of harangue overtly damning the
occupiers.

On June 30, 1941, there was a commotion in Brussels.
Everybody rushed outside to read a proclamation posted by our
beloved Mayor. It was plastered or rather glued on every blank
wall of the city.

The proclamation read:

City of Brussels
PROCLAMATION

My Dear Citizens,

The German Authorities told me that I have to resign and terminate my position as Mayor of the City of Brussels. The only avenue left to me is to obey their orders although it violates the Convention of The Hague and nothing in my conduct justifies this harsh measure taken against me. I was under the impression that I had served well and had accomplished multiple tasks, always heavy and sad, that are incumbent on the leader of a country while occupied by the enemy.

It was proposed and suggested that I continue my job, but the conditions under which I would have had to exercise my function as Mayor would have forced me to follow some laws dated April 16, 1941, which were in violation of laws dated May 10, 1940.

By accepting their offer to serve as mayor, I would be trampling on my honor and my duty and therefore disobeying the fundamental laws of our Country to which I had sworn obedience. I have refused and although there were rumors to the contrary, I have not left my prewar post and I have NOT resigned.

I AM AND WILL REMAIN THE ONE AND ONLY LEGITIMATE MAYOR OF THE CITY OF BRUSSELS.

The next and future Belgian authority named in my place and applying the above-mentioned laws will do so without legal foundation.

I bid you not "adieux" : but "au revoir."

I leave you temporarily I am asking you to bear your miseries and your material as well as moral sufferings with CALM, COURAGE and CONFIDENCE; I know that you will face life with a proud soul and a strong heart.

Anyone who belongs to our race fears nothing; nor anybody in the world : their only fear is to give up on their duty and lose their honor.

Remain united : your UNION will be your STRENGTH and will guarantee a better future.

< God will protect Belgium >
< And Her King. >

Mayor
Dr. F.J. VAN DE MEULEBROECK

City Hall, June 30, 1941.

I want to add that our motto is, "Union gives strength" and the last line of our anthem is, "God will protect Belgium and her King." These two were forbidden phrases during the occupation. Of course you may have guessed what happened to our heroic Mayor. He was under house arrest for the duration of the war. I don't remember worshipping or even liking any mayor of Brussels before him—except for Monsieur Max, but after that proclamation he attained sainthood.

— CHAPTER FOURTEEN —

Tightening Our Belts

One of the most important things for a teenager is FOOD. We were always at the receiving end of new and economical recipes. Everybody was skinny where I lived, and anybody that showed any increase in his or her girth or weight became immediately suspicious. We were dieting in unison. The question most often asked of thin Belgian women was, "Madame what has happened to your opulent bosom?" To which she would answer: "The Germans went away with it." To men the comments were less delicate, more like " Your neck looks like a turkey's." A few months into the occupation we found out that there was a street in Brussels where you could find any kind of food you craved at extravagant prices. The street was the Rue des Radis, and there you could buy butter, coffee, potatoes, dried beans, white flour, all the things that made life precious now and yet were so ordinary in peacetime. I never went to the Rue des Radis although it was located close to my school. This was commercialism of the worst kind. Later on I found out that papa was buying" black market" butter for his own use, sneaking it into his office at the Savings Bank. It was his way to compensate for the **vicissitudes** *(See vocabulary at back of book for all words that are in bold type.)* of life and his way to rationalize his fall from grace—from civil engineer to mere bank clerk. This had been humiliating to him, but the butter he sneaked in and shared with me was his consolation. I never told my mother or my siblings about my discovery. Papa and I tacitly agreed to keep this our secret.

For our family, *Rue des Radis* was out of the question. We didn't have the money to pay approximately $50.00 for a kilo of butter, but the people who could afford to pay those prices were not all collaborators or "Nazi friendly." Many had money. Belgium was a rich country before the war yet there also was a class of citizens that had made a lot of money selling soap on the black market during the First World War and they were the force behind the black market operation at *Rue des Radis.* The "Soap Barons" of WWI were at it again.

We used to dream of white bread, but flour was not available. Some times we could buy wheat grain on the black market and bring it home and grind it by hand on a small grinding machine. That was my reluctant brother's job. My father had fastened the hand-operated machine on a sturdy table and had placed the whole contraption in the garage. However, after seeing how hard it was for my brother to grind the wheat kernels and turn the crank by hand, papa decided to "go electric." He fastened a motor to the grinding thing with straps and metal hinges and fan belts and it looked rather professional. Brother Guy was delighted until he turned the switch on. The motor was so powerful that it sent table, grinding machine, and precious wheat grain, all over, almost taking my brother into the **maelstrom** it had created. Since the machine was made of cast iron, which happened to be breakable, you can imagine what had happened; but not to worry, Papa went to its rescue. He patched it so well with metal straps, screws, bolts, that made it look like an armored tank. I will never forget that machine and the way it looked after papa fixed it. In my mind it became comparable to a mutilated, bandaged war veteran, hobbling on crutches needing our respect and getting it. However, the electrification had broken and now poor Guy had to turn the crank once again, pushing the kernels into the funnel with a screwdriver to make them go down more easily.

My sister and I sifted the roughly ground wheat kernels to make the precious flour, but we had to make sure that it wasn't sifted too finely. We had to make it as coarse as possible, no waste permitted, and the by-product was excellent. It was whole-wheat flour at its best not to be compared to the oat kernels we had tried before. It didn't happen often that we could buy wheat in the rough because it was very expensive. But the time had come for us to find some farmer who would sell us the surplus that the Nazis let them keep for their own use. My grandfather after searching his memory remembered some old buddy who had a farm and lived close to Brussels. However, the good people spoke Flemish only (Belgians living in Brussels spoke French and Flemish; however, many Belgians in the north spoke only Flemish and many in the south spoke only French). Since I didn't speak Flemish very well, the expedition to their farm was reserved mainly to my brother who dabbled in Flemish and my grandmother who spoke Flemish fairly well.

The farm was located in Meerbeek, a two-mile walk from the streetcar terminal in Ninove. Once there, we had to socialize a bit and then find out what extras the farmers had. They used to sell us butter, bacon, or potatoes depending on availability. I went there a few times though because one of the farm boys had a crush on me and had called a newborn calf "Arlette" in my honor. I tried to speak Flemish with him, but he was a shy young boy. The most painful thing was going back home with the provisions that weighed a lot and facing that long walk back to the streetcar stop.

The Germans eventually found out about the farmers' selling the surplus to the people and didn't like it. They used to stop the streetcars, inspect the packages, confiscate our food, and either fine us or send us to jail. Therefore, we had to conceal the food we brought back. We heard fabulous tales of a lady who had hung a slab of bacon between her legs, under a full skirt. Tales too of boys hiding butter under their caps. Oops, I borrowed that one from Tom Sawyer. Tales of potatoes being put in ladies' bloomers, which had once again become fashionable, circulated.

We even heard of a man who went to get provisions armed with two suitcases and his German shepherd dog. He had bought a half pig and had put the meat in one suitcase keeping the other one empty. At the sight of a German patrol, he would sneak the dog into the empty suitcase and when the soldier would ask what he had in it, he would reply honestly, "My dog," which of course the patrolmen would not believe. Then the police would renew his request and open the suitcase while looking at his prey with daggers in his eyes and then he would be totally surprised to be either licked or bitten by the confined dog. The patrolman never inquired about the content of the other suitcase being glad to be rid of the suspect.

My father once brought home a whole fresh ham, which my mother cooked. However, because it was huge we had to conserve it carefully. We hung it in the bathroom vent, a cool place—free of bugs, but not as cold as a refrigerator. It was fine until days later when the meat started to taste like cheese. We finally got rid of it when it started moving. Maggots had taken residence near the bone but I think that Pelot scraped them out, rinsed it and ate the rest of the ham. Once again, Pelot to the rescue.

We also tried to grow our own veggies. Since our neighborhood was being planned and built, the sidewalks had not been completed. Space between the curb and the uncompleted sidewalk gave us the opportunity to grow something there. Moreover, Papa decided to cultivate the vacant lot next to our house. Not only *How to Raise Chickens for Dummies* hadn't been written yet, but also its companion *How to Grow Vegetables for Dummies* hadn't been written either. So papa went to his favorite bookstore and bought the most complicated and convoluted guide on how to raise tomatoes, potatoes, onions, carrots, etc. that you could find. But we tilled the clay, sowed the seeds, planted the tomatoes and whatever we planted grew. Papa later sent me his book when I bought a house in the country and had plans to cultivate a garden.

The Belgians cultivate a lot of sugar beets, which becomes cattle **fodder** after the extraction of the sap, which in turn is used in making sugar. That crop also found its way to Germany, and sugar became heavily rationed although we were allotted a bigger ration during July and August, permitting us to make jelly and preserves for the winter. Our cravings for sugar, as well as our appetite for candy, had to be curbed because both were absolutely unavailable. However, papa found an article in some publication stating that if you were a beekeeper in good standing you were permitted to obtain twenty kilos of sugar as bee food. My father immediately applied for his ration of sugar, which was given him without even having a bee inspector check the states of the hives or their number.

Papa was raising phantom bees in phantom hives, and he was smiling with utter joy at his own cunning and licking his chops in anticipation of tasting sugar again. My mother didn't share his enthusiasm, wondering how he was going to get out of an eventual inspection by the bee people, unable to show the authorities that the bees were just a ploy to get sugar. Oh, but papa was ahead of her. He had been studying bees and bee diseases and was ready to tell the inspectors that the bees had a disease called *Loque* and not only had the bees had to be destroyed but the hives as well since the *Loque* was such a virulent affliction that it threatened the lives of all bees in the country. So papa was especially happy to have hoodwinked the enemy once again.

The task of getting the sugar fell on us, girls, so Ginette and I gladly obliged since we were promised an extra ration. We walked the ten miles to the destination and were given the heaviest bags of sugar that we could carry. It was deadly hot that day and the ten kilos might have been one hundred pounds that we each had to carry. We finally made it home, and papa used a teaspoon of the famous sugar to put on his strawberries. After one bite he got up gagging, grabbing his throat with his hands and spat the whole thing into the kitchen sink.

This famous sugar was mixed with sand but that didn't deter papa from counter attacking the problem. He melted the sugar in water, hoping for the sand to sink to the bottom of the container so he could harvest the sweet water and eventually crystallize the sugar by evaporation. We found out to our chagrin that the water was turning pale purple and after a thorough analysis, we found out the sugar contained the chemical aniline and therefore was unfit for human consumption. Now we understood why the "bee people" had appeared to be so lax when we put in the application; they knew all along that we were going to be fooled into believing we were going to fool them. We had tried and it had not worked out, but papa was not defeated. What will come next, we wondered?

As soon as my brother came home from school he would rush to the kitchen and search the food locker for something to eat. But that was strictly forbidden and considered stealing since all our food was divided equally among the five of us. Nobody was entitled to eat more than his or her share. But Guy had developed the knack of talking with his mouth full; therefore, if my mother asked him a question without seeing him, he could answer her perfectly normally as if his mouth were empty. Yet my mother smelled a rat and sought to catch him in the act of stealing using clever methods of detection, but it had to be done quickly in order not to arouse his suspicion. She finally found the right thing to do and commanded him abruptly, "Guy, whistle." That he could not do with food in his mouth, so he was caught eating OUR food. And from that day on the door between the dining room and the living room had to remain open when we came back from school.

Hunger was terrible to experience day after day. Sometimes the food we ate was of unknown origin. For example, we never knew what kind of flour was used in the bread we bought at the bakery. I believe that it was made from a variety of grains almost unfit for human consumption and we also knew that in order to cheat us the baker added an inordinate amount of water in the preparation of the bread, which increased its weight and made it hard to keep from spoiling. After two days the bread was moldy—my father swore it glowed in the dark, yet we never hesitated about eating it. Throwing out food was unthinkable.

We found out soon enough that the Great Reich needed coal and plenty of it. Therefore, we were unable to buy coal from our prewar supplier. Instead we had to burn wood, which became very expensive and hard to find. Furthermore, the wood we bought was sold by the ton or fraction thereof and the merchants used to deliver the logs soaking wet. After a few days the ton of wood had shrunk to half its size.

We were also unable to use our central heating system. The coal-burning furnace required too much wood; therefore, we had to use space stoves and hook them up to the fireplace. Then wood became scarce and we were forced to buy some kind of wet coal dust mixed with mud that when ignited smelled of rotten eggs.

That pseudo coal was called *schlam*. Usually we were able to ignite it after a series of unsuccessful attempts. The warmth it radiated was minimal; the stoves were not big enough to heat our apartment, and our bedrooms had no heat at all. After having known a rather comfortable existence before the war, this cold was hard to bear.

As in every big city we had city gas, which became regulated by the enemy. It was given full strength two hours a day, between 7:00 AM and 8:00 AM and between 6:00 PM and 7:00 PM. In between there was not enough pressure to amount to anything; then after a short while the pressure died down altogether. The two hours per day rationing stayed the same for a few months until it was changed again. Then it became available every other day for one hour in the morning one day, and one hour at night the next.

We had a cooking stove in the kitchen that used wood, but it was hooked to a corner chimney which lacked the draft necessary for good combustion, but at least it was an alternative to gas cooking. And then papa once again had an idea that was worth a cool million. He discovered that if you placed an electric space heater on its back, took off the protective grill and put a different kind of resistance—the kind you found in an electric hot plate—replaced the grill, keeping the space heater on its back, you found yourself the proud owner of a great electric range more stable and stronger than a flimsy hot plate. With the help of my sister, he turned out a lot of these and sold them to the grateful Belgians.

Our German tenants had plenty of coal and they used it in their private furnace but that didn't help us. They soon found out that their furnace was hooked on to our bedroom radiators upstairs, and they had the pipes cut off immediately. It felt as though our last contact with our previous life of comfort had been ripped away from us.

— Chapter Fifteen —

More Deprivations, More Anger

After food, coal and other basic necessities, we needed clothes.
It was sad to outgrow the clothes we had and have to wear
the same clothes for years, but worse yet those were now
starting to show their age. For fashion-conscious Belgians this was
devastating. Soon whatever material we had accumulated before the
war was gone or had been used up some way. So we began to make
skirts from papa's trousers. The seat of his pants was shiny and
therefore discarded, but the leg part was the part we used. After we
had ripped the seams and turned the material inside out, we could
make a decent skirt for either my sister or me.

During the war the winters happened to be unusually cold and
wool materials were not to be found. Since winter coats were not
available in stores any more, the resourceful Belgians came up with
a winner of an idea. If a blanket kept you warm at night, why not
use them to fashion something to keep you warm in the daytime?
Let's make overcoats with them. The rationale behind the idea was
simple: if you were missing your blanket at night, you could always
use your coat as a blanket. Winter blankets were made from virgin
wool and were incredibly warm and comfortable. Unfortunately
many blankets were dyed a light color and sported stripes crosswise.
We had the drycleaner dye the blankets a darker color but still the
stripes showed through and everybody could see that our coats had
once been keeping us warm in bed. Some mean kids made fun of
us, but we didn't care as long as we were warm. Still, I felt
humiliated by the remarks, but my mother told us not to care.

Silk stockings were the next luxury to become extinct.
Before the war, women wore silk stockings, which were expensive
and rather fragile. They were not discarded as easily as nylon
stockings are now and had to be repaired by special people who
would re-knit the runs by picking the stitches one at a time all
the way up the ladder. They used to charge you one franc per
run, which was cheaper than having to buy a new pair. If you
couldn't afford to pay for the repairs, you had to do it yourself

and spend hours re-weaving the runs one stitch at a time sometimes for the whole length of the stocking. Some lasted for the whole duration of the war. Needless to say, silk stockings were not part of my daily wear.

I was still wearing knitted woolen knee socks and I had learned how to reweave the holes in the toes and in the heel. My big toe was a poker and I was constantly obliged to reweave the puncture it made. We used to slip a wooden egg inside the stocking, and the curved and smooth surface of the egg would enable us to weave the hole with special wool. I loved to do that, as a matter of fact it was a skill taught in Home Economics. For the more sophisticated girls, it became fashionable to paint their legs with a special paint that gave their legs that matte look that only silk stockings could produce. The product was called *bas liquide* (pronounced in French ba-likeed) but we called it *"basslikwid,"* to give it an American consonance. This sounded more distinguished, elegant, progressive, and modern. Some girls even drew a seam at the back of their legs with eyeliner giving "the stockings" a more realistic look. At that time stockings had seams at the back that were supposed to be straight.

We exchanged clothes with friends and family of course, and many used to sell their cast off dresses and suits. Shoes were a different matter. They were very hard to find, so they were worn until they became full of holes and too shabby to give away or sell. Furthermore, the corner cobblers were running out of leather with which to resole shoes, so they had to find another way to make a living. Someone invented a pliable and **articulated** wooden sole; however, the top of the shoe was made of cloth and fashioned to look like loafers. The lining of the shoes was made of cardboard, which would become detached from the cloth and walking became a torture. But, as I said before, the hinged soles facilitated walking.

Maurice Chevalier even sang a song, "Click-clack make our wooden soles." Poor Maurice Chevalier, a beloved singer before the war, lost a lot of his luster by performing publicly during the occupation. To many, he was considered a traitor and an opportunist. In fact Chevalier at first refused to perform in Germany but later agreed, as did other French artists, such as

Edith Piaf. The Germans agreed to release ten prisoners, so Chevalier—without a fee—entertained 3000 prisoners. After the war he was accused of collaboration but his name was cleared. He then regained an even greater popularity.

In fact, Chevalier did more than sing to prisoners: during the Nazi occupation of France, Chevalier had hidden his Jewish girlfriend and her parents, at great risk to himself.

We used to make summer dresses out of bed sheets and I even made myself a dress using some old draperies of my grandmother's. And I hadn't even seen the movie *Gone with the Wind* yet. In order to make a statement and render the sheets more elegant, we used to trim the dresses with embroidery or buttons and all kinds of adornment. My grandmother found a piece of navy blue wool stashed away somewhere among other treasures, a rather stiff serge, but there was enough to make a blazer, which I desperately needed. My dear grandmother gave me the material, and I had the blazer tailored by a professional. In order to be finished properly the jacket had to be lined but lining material was not available. My grandfather used to be an undertaker and still possessed a piece of purple silk used to line men's coffins. There was no other alternative but to line my brand new blazer with the purple silk. I kept that blazer buttoned up at all times, come rain or come shine, not only was violet a bad match with navy blue, but I was sure that people would immediately detect that the lining of my jacket had been destined to line an unfortunate man's coffin.

It became imperative to find ways to renew our wardrobes with the clothes we already possessed and breathe new life into the old garments. We started by taking an old skirt, carefully undoing the hem, ripping the old seams, and turning the old skirt inside out and would re-sew them on the other side. The wrong side of the skirt became the right side now and since it had never seen the light of day was thus brighter and newer looking than the outside. An added bonus: the threadbare or shiny appearance was less noticeable once it was turned inside out. Furthermore, it gave work to the seamstresses who were quite idle during that time. I remember wearing a turned inside-out coat, navy blue before the war but plaid on the reverse side during the war.

As for the men, they had their frayed shirt collars simply turned around, but that was a practice dating from the Great Depression and was continued even in the United States. But human ingenuity went even further; it became fashionable for some men to wear detachable "celluloid" collars (celluloid was another precursor of plastic), which buttoned to their collarless shirt. Those collars were easy to clean and in that period of restrictions it was easier to quickly wash the collar under running water. As for the rest of the shirt? Soap was at a premium; therefore, the rest of the shirt remained on the body for a trifle longer. The challenge was to make clothes last longer and at the same time maintain an elegant and affluent appearance.

We also used the rabbits. After we ate them for dinner, Papa tanned the skins of our rabbits, and we learned to make collars and cuffs from the fur. The finished product was sewn to the dyed blanket coats, and we looked like a million marks. I must add that the fur of our rabbits was silky and lovely and the colors always matched our garments.

While some of us were refurbishing our wardrobes, we noticed that after a while the more adventurous and wealthy of our friends started to show up with clothes that were totally out of the ordinary. Their whole demeanor was changed from their hair to their shoes. The young men's hair was long and coiffed in a sort of pompadour but slicker than Elvis's a few years later. Their pinstriped trousers were narrow; their shoes, heavy; and they wore very loose tweed jackets and thin and narrow ties. The girls wore very short skirts, tailored shirts, and heavy shoes and like the boys, they wore long and oversized tweed jackets. That fashion seemed to be emanating from France and those young people were called *Les Zazous.* Later on I found out they were the equivalent of the American Zoot Suits; hence ZAZOO; hence *Les Zazous.* Papa found them terribly decadent, but I envied them with all my heart.

They also danced to music that papa found revolting but I found fascinating. Those young people had their own music and gestures; they danced twirling their index fingers above their heads. I never knew where those young people bought those clothes, but after all we could find anything on the black market providing we had the money and the connections. That strange

music was Swing, a by product of jazz, the precursor of Rock and
Roll, which came directly from the United States, and in direct
opposition to the military music and martial marches the Third
Reich relished. It was another form of rebellion by young people
across Europe to show their contempt for the occupier.[9]
    We were also introduced to the exhilarating rhythm of Duke
Ellington, Benny Goodman, and other greats of the Jazz period.
And pretty soon—to the irritation of the Nazis—we had embraced
that delightful sound. French musicians didn't remain idle,
increasing the popularity of the "Hot Club de France" in Brussels.
    Jazz had the taste of forbidden fruit. Great musicians were
making the scene. Django Reinhardt, Stephane Grapelli, and Alix
Combelle had a following unheard of before the war. Young
people were going crazy. Although the Nazis considered jazz a
decadent product of "convulsive negroes from New Orleans and
Jewish businessmen of Broadway"(*Les Zazous*, Jean-Claude
Loiseau), they permitted the French Radio Stations to play the
music but without the lyrics. As soon as Louis Armstrong, for
example, started to sing, the technicians or disc jockey was forced
to **shunt** the sound. The press nicknamed the young jazz
enthusiasts *Les petits Swings*, but in order to enable American
music to be played on Radio Paris, "St. Louis Blues " became "*La
Tristesse de Saint Louis*"; "Tiger Rag" was baptized "*La Rage du
Tigre*"; thus they were accepted by the Chief of Propaganda and
passed censorship. Of course when America joined the allies,
American Music was banned, but not to worry, all the good songs
had already been translated into French.

— CHAPTER SIXTEEN —

Car Troubles

A few weeks after the German invasion anyone owning a car
had to turn it in to the authorities or hide it in a garage if
possible. Papa refused to turn his car in and had the
audacity to park it on the side of the house because he needed his

garage for other endeavors; he was always inventing something. A few weeks after papa parked his car by the house, some desperado stole the tires, even the wheels and left the invalid auto to decay slowly but surely by the side of our house. It was hard for papa to give up driving; he hated waiting around for a streetcar and it was a real heartbreak for him to do without his beloved automobile.

None of our friends were permitted to drive their cars. Gasoline was unavailable and delivery trucks were equipped with some contraption that used to burn diesel fuel. The diesel fuel was replaced by a wood burning contraption but that also proved to be so inefficient that it was replaced by *gasogene*, an ersatz gas sold in cylindrical tanks. The cylinder of *gasogene* was strapped to the roof of the cars, emitting black smoke as well as a disagreeable smell. We were afraid the Nazis had invented a gasoline replacement but *gasogene* lacked the energy to reach decent speeds. The few foreigners who were allowed to drive their cars were neutral nationals such as the Swiss or Swedes. Medical doctors had permission to drive their cars providing they equipped them with the *gasogene* contraption. Only Germans were permitted gasoline. Our beloved Clydesdale horses were called back into action once more and helped the **collier** deliver his **ersatz** coal and water soaked firewood to our door.

We had to either walk or take public transportation, in itself not too bad, except that the last streetcar stopped running after 10:00 PM (or 9:00 PM if we had been bad and were being punished by the Nazis). Buses were not running anymore, just streetcars running between 6:00 AM to 10:00 PM, using electricity. Many German soldiers were also using our public transportation.

We were immediately ordered to observe black out procedures, which meant that we were obliged by law to darken our windows at nightfall by putting up totally opaque drapes. Cars were not allowed to use their bright beams at night. As a matter of fact the headlights were covered with black paint with only a slit used to project a feeble ray of light. There were no streetlights and no lights in department store windows. At dusk and night the whole town was uninviting, dipped in black, and to add insult to injury we were not allowed to gather with our friends anywhere. More than three young men talking together got under the Nazis' skin. They were always listening to the conversations and misunderstanding what was being talked about. Our friend, Erice Moray, was talking with his buddies about a football game that had taken place the day before when he casually mentioned that his team was a bunch of losers. A German heard the last part of the conversation and totally misunderstood what was being said; he thought Erice was making derogatory remarks about the Germans and criticizing the regime. So they immediately took Erice to the Gestapo accusing him of talking against the Reich and forced him, stark naked, to sweep the offices of the *Gestapo*. They took pleasure in stripping people of their dignity. Not only was it incredibly demeaning to be naked there, sweeping the floor, but women were working in the office and were not sparing of their comments.

Girls were permitted to get together more readily than guys. We would meet at what used to be a pastry shop for an ice cream made with skimmed milk and just the taste of that ice cream, brimming with ice crystals, made me shiver. The ice cream was never served in a cone—we had no flour to make cones—so the ice cream was served in a metal dish that made the "ice cream" even colder than it had to be. Our hang out was named "The *Bouquet Romain*" because the pseudo ice cream was Italian in flavor and shape.

There was beer, one of the most famous beverages of the Belgians. Surprise—that also had been diluted to such an extent that it was nicknamed *pisse tout de suite zero huit*. The first word of the quotation gives you a hint as to what it meant to us. Sometimes our little family used to go down town to a nice café, which permitted its customers to bring their own food and wash it down with the weak brew they were selling. Genuine restaurants were closed, except for a few that catered to German officers. Our Brussels was deprived of the smells of the fine cuisine that had made her famous. No lights, no smells, no taste, no cars, no music, no joy, no freedom.

— CHAPTER SEVENTEEN —

Ouija Board 101

We needed distractions from the occupation. One of those was movies. The few movies that were palatable were a few French films. We stayed away from German flicks altogether—too much propaganda, and their sense of humor was not tailored to our taste. One French film stood out during that time—*Les Visiteurs du Soir (The Night Visitors)*—that told the story of a castle that had been captured by an allegorical enemy. The film told the story of two musicians, emissaries of the devil, sent to disrupt the wedding of Baron Hughes' daughter and her fiancé Hugh Renaud. The allegorical enemy is the devil. The film appeared to be a pure romantic fantasy, but it really disguised a hidden meaning. Furthermore, the film was set in medieval times to keep away from the contemporary settings and times, so no one would confuse the make believe with sad reality. There were some incredible sound effects that gave the film an air of drama and anticipation. To us of course the castle symbolized France; the occupants, the allies; the allegorical enemy—the devil—depicted the Germans. The Germans never caught on and let us enjoy the film they never could understand. I suppose it was too subtle.

Another distraction was games such as MONOPOLY and the OUIJA board. We used to get together with friends at our house and play MONOPOLY, the "in" game, or we used to play records and dance to the music, mostly American jazz. And then one day out of nowhere and out of desperation to find a new way of entertainment, we discovered the OUIJA board. I can't remember who proposed it but papa made a OUIJA set under the guidance of a newfound friend, Marcel Mostade. The game consisted of a cardboard sheet and a thin wooden plank the size of a hand. On the cardboard were printed the letters of the alphabet, under which were the 0 to 9 numerals, and the word YES on the right side and NO on the left. Between the YES and NO papa had put a big question mark. Papa also fashioned the small wooden plank. The object of the whole thing was to be able to contact the dead, or rather its spirit, asking clever questions. The spirit would in turn dictate its thought through the plank. In time of war finding dead souls was not a difficult task; the harvest was plentiful.

The next step, which was more tricky, was to unearth a medium, someone who had the power to make the OUIJA plank move all by itself. The plank would guide the hand and point to the letters, one at a time. Someone would write down the letters that strangely enough would form words; the plank would stop briefly between words, and then we would record and decipher the message it spelled out.

I became the medium in spite of myself. My ability even to this day hasn't been explained. I had barely put my hand on the wooden board, when it would start moving, pointing to the letters. I swore that it went all by itself; as a matter of fact, sometimes my hand didn't even touch the little *planchette*. Marcel Mostade, the instigator, was well versed in spiritualism and had a knack of asking questions that were answered by the fast moving little plank under my hand. I don't know where the answers were coming from but the little board moved fast and furiously and I had a hard time keeping up with its speed. Was it coincidence? Was it something else? All I know, it was weird. The answers were troubling sometimes. Even my father who was a cynic of the worst kind was impressed by my skill or my GIFT. The answers the plank spelled out made a big impression on many.

Sometimes Marcel (who spoke English like a pro because he had spent his childhood in England during World War I) would ask the questions in English because we were communicating with dead British soldiers as well as Belgians. I would give the answers in English, a language barely formed in my brain at that time. Papa who had always considered me to be a scatterbrain made a one eighty and elevated me to a force to be reckoned with. We used to connect with a favorite spirit called Popol who used to give us advice on how to live, die, and treat one another. He told us that dead spirits surrounded us, and when in shock, papa asked if any German spirits were hanging around? Popol replied, wisely, "YES, dead is dead, isn't it?"

Spiritualism became our main pastime. And I remember one night Popol telling us to be very careful, that German soldiers were patrolling our street, zeroing in, and fining people who hadn't properly blackened their windows. He told us that we were at risk; that very instant the bell rang loudly sending us in a tizzy. We answered the door to be told by German soldiers that light was seen around the window and that we had to remedy the situation immediately. I swear that I hadn't heard any noise coming from the street. Coincidence? Maybe . . . and how about the time Popol told us that King Boris of Bulgaria had died at the precise moment Popol was OUIJA-ing with us and the radio wasn't even on. Coincidence? And the next day when we found out that in reality King Boris had died; we were stunned. Popol had told us also that the Nazis had assassinated him and that his heart attack was a Nazi invention. WE KNEW! Another time Popol told us that we were about to be bombed by our allies, and there were twenty-five bombers flying above, although everything was quiet and peaceful and we couldn't even hear the dull sound of the plane engines. My father told Popol that he was mistaken, yet at that very moment the sirens started to screech and we were forced to take shelter in our basement. Popol scored again. Coincidence?

At the beginning of our spiritualism period we were still speaking to the Heumanns upstairs, and Mrs. H. became fascinated by the OUIJA board. We had to be very, very careful. We had to tell Popol to desist, to keep away, when she was with us. We did tricks: Mrs. Heumann would go upstairs in her apartment and scribble a word on a piece of paper while I remained downstairs trying to figure out the word she had written and try to spell it out with my magic plank. That was rough but it happened, I guessed the word. I can't remember what the word was, but after that session, I had such a headache that it almost became our last séance.

I was enjoying a fame that was difficult to resist; however, my teachers in school were not satisfied with my poor grades, so I had to cut down on my psychic activities and come back to earth, so to speak. I don't know what we would have done without the OUIJA board. The board helped us to spend some mighty fine evenings.

Our house became a hub, papa was impressed, and above all Ouija-ing didn't cost us a dime. We checked on Popol, and the curriculum vitae he had given us came out exactly as he had told us. We checked with parents, friends, and neighbors and found that Popol, born in Brussels, had been killed at the beginning of the war. We verified his address. Coincidence? Papa was VERY impressed. *"C'est probant"* (it's verifiable). The most popular question asked by the neophytes to Popol was, " When will the war end?" To which Popol would reply that he was not a prophet that he was sent to help people make a transition between life and death. WEIRD! We really enjoyed our séances, which lasted until the end of the war. It is strange to see how something as far fetched as spiritualism can unite desperate people. We were all grasping for something that could eventually make sense and ease our pains and desperate state of mind. We needed to be reassured that this was a temporary situation, that the war would end, and that the best thing next to God was dear old Popol, our guiding light from "outer" wherever. We later found out that the Catholic Church forbade spiritualism so we didn't bother to tell *Monsieur le Cure* in the privacy of the confessional.

— CHAPTER EIGHTEEN —

Arrested

As days went by it became increasingly difficult to accustom ourselves to our new life. Schools started to change their schedules in response to the children's health; they were becoming weaker. So we started school at 9:00AM instead of 8:00AM. However, we were determined to go to school just to defy the occupier. They had closed the schools during World War I, but this time we wanted to be educated just to be contrary. However, we had to follow the rules. For example, my principal, Miss Vanvolsem, forbade any display of patriotism for fear of retaliation by the enemy. She was determined not to have her school closed, and we were not to complain about anything.

My brother went to a private school, all boys, and dutifully brought my father's newsletters to be distributed to his classmates.

And then one day two trench-coated Gestapo agents entered my brother's school and demanded to see Guy in his classroom. They entered the room, called my brother's name, "*Herr deMonceau*," which they pronounced "*de Monkow*," Guy rose from his seat. Without further ado they asked him to produce his school bag, then full of the prohibited newspapers. My brother without hesitation seized a schoolmate's empty satchel and showed it to the *Gestapo* who examined and found it empty, yet they took him to their headquarters anyway since he was irritating the Gestapo by his denials. In that regime you were guilty until you proved your innocence.

But just to make sure the Gestapo men went to my house to tell my parents that their son had been passing underground papers, so they wanted to investigate the premises. The very first thing they did upon entering my house was to turn on the radio to find out if it had been tuned to the BBC. We knew that if it had been tuned to the British Radio Station we would have been in trouble. They searched my father's office downstairs; they then proceeded to search my parents' apartment. After a fruitless search they demanded to see our rooms, located on the fourth floor. For some strange reason, they bypassed my brother's room; the door was closed and they didn't bother to open it. Instead they went straight to our room, the girls' room, and did a methodical search. They didn't find anything in our room either but that didn't matter. They arrested my brother by proxy, ordering him to appear in front of the Gestapo for questioning. I found out later that he was questioned at our regular Court House—*Le Palais de Justice*.

Guy was only fifteen years old and was not exactly the athletic type. As a matter of fact he was rather small for his age and certainly did not pose any kind of a threat to the Nazi regime. He was a mild mannered young fellow. Nevertheless he went in front of a tribunal and was condemned to one-month imprisonment. My mother attended the mock trial, held at our Belgian Court of Justice in Brussels, now run by the Nazis. Mother urged my brother to "please defend himself." Of course no lawyers represented him. He was just a kid, yet it would have been the same scenario for anybody who had committed a mild infraction.

On the appointed day, September 7, 1941, my parents took

him to Saint Gilles Prison, nicknamed The Patriots' Hotel. He had been condemned to a one month in prison, but with the Nazis you could not always predict. My mother had assembled as much food (tidbits) as she could find and had made a small packet for him to take to jail. I remember my mother putting a piece of gingerbread in this little packet. We were glad to let him take it, since we knew that Saint Gilles Prison was not exactly the Ritz. A few days prior to his incarceration, Guy had gone to the prison and had inquired about rules and regulations. The sergeant in charge told my brother to bring some food and a blanket. My parents had the fabulous idea of taking a photo of my brother right in front of the prison. He was carrying the famous car-blanket, referred to as PLAID, nicknamed *Verte-verte*, because of its dark green and black tartan plaid.

That blanket had been used by us through all our illnesses and had a very special meaning to us children. Made of some comfy rayon plush with a Scottish tartan pattern, the blanket had been used specifically to keep automobile passengers warm in the days before cars were equipped with heaters. These blankets became obsolete but had been very fashionable at the turn of the twentieth century, and my father had had the opportunity to buy one for us. In the picture you can see Guy carrying the famous blanket.

The prison had a forbidding appearance. The massive door would give you chills and the turrets at the five corners of the huge building were not welcoming. The prison consisted of five wings built spoke-wise around the central hub. One wing served as a military prison for Nazi servicemen, another wing was reserved for thieves and civilian criminals, and the last three wings harbored political prisoners. Prisoners entered through a small door carved into the huge double door. The threshold that was not level with the sidewalk forced them to lift their feet before entering. Guy was swallowed by the darkness inside that medieval looking building, disappearing from my parents' view. He was taken to a cell by a soldier, who slammed the door behind him.

My brother shared his cell with two other men who had been there for a while and who very quickly convinced my brother to divide his little bag of goodies with them; after all, they rationalized," You know how long you'll be here; we don't know

where and when we'll be out." The concrete cell had no iron bars
as do its American counterparts. A metal door was equipped with
a pass through, from which the prisoners received their morning
ration of bread. At night, the prisoners were allotted some soup,
but at that time the door was opened and the soup was poured by
a civilian prisoner called in German a *fatick*, under the supervision

of a Nazi soldier. The prisoners were allowed to exercise in the prison yard once in a while; that is, they were allowed to walk single file around and around the yard. No talking was permitted. To enforce this, a soldier stood in the middle of the walking prisoners, who, by the way, were wearing their own clothes; no uniforms were issued them. A soldier supervised the prisoners who despite the scrutiny managed to send and to receive messages using signs or making noises at certain intervals. My brother even made the acquaintance of a British soldier who had been caught hiding in Brussels and was detained in a political jail waiting to be sent to a *stalag* in Germany.

We were not allowed to visit my brother but once a fortnight (a two week period). We were permitted to send him a one-page letter, which he was not allowed to answer. At the end of his sentence our brother, now an official political prisoner, came home without fanfare. We knew then that we were going to be on the Nazis' black list. Nonetheless, we were delighted to see him again especially as he was coming back carrying the famous blanket, *verte-verte*.

— CHAPTER NINETEEN —
The Underground

The situation in Brussels became tenser as the days went by. My friend Angele came to school one day in a terribly agitated state. She asked me to swear to keep a secret, telling me that her brother's friends, the Eagle Scouts that my sister and I had been raving about, had been arrested by the Gestapo and were to be executed the next day. They had been caught hiding and passing weapons, a crime that the Nazis did not forgive. They ordered their execution without the benefit of trial or long-term imprisonment. The most horrendous fact is that we heard the rifle shots that killed them.

We were living close to the place where the Nazis executed the rebels at dawn. Almost every week we would be awakened by the sound of shots, the murder of another patriot. Now I knew for sure what the young men were talking about and why they always talked in hushed tones. They belonged to the underground, the *maquis*. Angele's brother, Marcel, thank goodness, hadn't been caught but disappeared altogether, joining the underground we assumed. This made my brother very envious, he dreamed of escaping and joining the free forces. This would be a very difficult endeavor. The escapees had to get in touch with professionals who would sneak them out of Belgium by ways and means very appealing to young people. Because travel was not permitted outside, very often they had to cross the French border in a hearse, a dump truck, or other mode of transport. However, once they crossed the border successfully, they would try to reach the French Non-Occupied Zone and more specifically Vichy, its capital.

Once in the Non-Occupied Zone, after making contact with the underground, they hoped to be sent to Spain. And that in itself was very dangerous. They had to be sure that their contact was legitimate or else if they were caught they were imprisoned and sent back to Belgium where they were given to the German authorities. In any case they had to traverse France and from there try to reach Spain across the Pyrenees Mountains, which are very high and dangerous to cross. Many men didn't make it. The ones that reached Spain on the other side of the Pyrenees had to be on constant alert. They had been escorted by Basque scouts through the designated mountain passes. The Spaniards were on the look out for defectors, as they were called, and because the Spaniards were allies of Hitler they automatically put the escapees into a concentration camp at *Miranda de Pampelona*. Once there they generally were detained for a while and were released at random with money provided by the British Government. The men were then permitted to cross the Portuguese border and stay at Coimbra University's campus in semi-seclusion. With the Portuguese government's approval, they were released a few at a time and permitted to sail to England. Angele's brother never gave his parents a hint about where he was going nor if he had made it to England. He was afraid to put his parents in jeopardy, so they had no idea of his whereabouts.

— CHAPTER TWENTY —

The United States Enters the War

The allies now had started to regroup and we heard with exhilaration that the United States had joined the cause. The US had weapons. They had planes and above all plenty of gasoline. Now the Allies possessed all the things that were in short supply before. Oh, we were almost in heaven. So the allies started to use those planes to bomb the military installations and the railroads all over Europe. The sirens blared all the time but this time the bombs falling from the sky were bits of freedom falling from heaven.

At the first sign of planes flying above, we would cheer and send kisses and scream with happiness. This made the Germans furious. After dancing in the street, we would reluctantly descend to the shelters. Every cellar and underground passage became an air raid shelter whose walls were fortified by sandbags. Sandbags were placed in front of low windows and over the grates of the coal chutes. As a precaution against broken panes and flying glass we taped the windows, using a criss-cross pattern. Although we all were in danger of being buried alive in those shelters, we were elated knowing that the allies were working toward our liberation. Yet despite all the dangers surrounding our daily activities and the menace of constant herding to those abominable air raid shelters, we tried to follow our pre-war routines.

— CHAPTER TWENTY-ONE —

The Opera Revolt

My parents, worried about our cultural education, bought us season tickets to the opera, which was still being performed. So the three of us, Ginette, Guy, and I went to the opera *Carmen*. The theater was crawling with uniformed Germans, many of them officers. I would say that the soldiers formed eighty percent of the assembly. *Carmen* by the French composer Georges Bizet was sung in French. As a matter of fact the operas in Belgium at that time were always sung in French, never in their original language. Anyway, Carmen, a gypsy, lured her lover, Don Jose, a captain in the army with a fine reputation, to the mountains where he would live with thieves and brigands. She clamored that once in the mountains he would be free, and she emphasized the word *freedom* in very lovely arias.

My brother hearing the word *freedom* became frantic. He stood up, clapping violently in midsong, clamoring for freedom, yelling, "We want our freedom." The Germans, totally ignorant of what was going on, believing they were following a Belgian tradition, stood up and started to clap until someone told them to stop immediately. This was an act of defiance. Then the hunt was on for my brother who, guessing the outcome, had vacated the premises in very high spirits. *Carmen* was canceled, never again played during the German occupation.

The same thing happened again one month later at the production of *Herodias*, a tragic opera by the French composer Jules Massenet. In this opera, Salome urges John the Baptist to flee to freedom. At which point my incorrigible brother stood up, and at the utterance of the word *freedom*, did the same thing as he had done with *Carmen*: he yelled *"freedom."* This opera was also swarming with Germans who did exactly as the others had done before, except that in this case my brother didn't wait for the opera to end but escaped before all hell could break lose. *Herodias* was also never played anymore during the occupation.

Belgium's history of revolution began at the opera. Long ago, before becoming free and being declared an autonomous country, Belgium had been a part of Holland. In 1830, the Belgians revolted against the Dutch, demanding independence. The revolution started at the opera house when a heart wrenching song aroused the patriotism of the audience. At the utterance of that very forceful song, the Belgians were up in arms, chasing the Hollanders, digging out the streets' cobblestones, and even pouring boiling oil on the retreating Dutch. In the end the Belgians won their independence. I guess some Germans had heard about that little piece of history and didn't want a repeat performance.

— CHAPTER TWENTY-TWO —
Papa Terrorizes the Renters

The German armies were all over the place—in Europe, Russia, and North Africa. Their fighting front was extended far and wide to the joy of my father who could smell disaster. He even approached our tenant, Mr. Heumann, to share his opinion. However, Heumann denied my father's prediction, saying the Hitler knew what he was doing. Ha! Ha! Ha! The mood of the Nazis was not upbeat. They were nervous.

Around this time Madame Heumann gave birth to a little girl and hired a maid to take care of the two little girls. The maid was Belgian, a disgusting turncoat who spoke French and could understand what we would say and translate it to the Heumanns. She was very young, with a pinched, little fox face, and rather tiny. She was to occupy the guest room on the fourth floor, next to our bedroom. She hated us because we didn't exactly approve of the fact that she was working for the enemy.

This was the end of 1941 and the weather was not cooperating with our miseries. It was cold and although our climate is usually rather moderate, this time winter was incredibly cold. Since we were unable to use our central heating because of the shortage of fuel, our water pipes froze. We had to get water from our neighbors and bring it back home in buckets, pots, pans, and bottles. Because our neighbors' houses were not close to our house this became tedious work. After a few days of intense cold the pipes going out of the house froze up as well. Upstairs the Germans were not bothered since they could use their furnace and the water upstairs. However, because of the condition of our pipes, all their waste spilled into our toilets that then overflowed into the hallway and onto the stairs. Believe me, the smell was intolerable. We politely asked our tenants to refrain from flushing their toilets, but the spiteful maid didn't cooperate and threatened to denounce us to the Gestapo. She suspected my father of writing the newsletters and she knew we were listening to the BBC. She told her boss, Mr. Heumann, that my father was a dangerous individual. After confronting Mr. Heumann, a terrible fight ensued, and my father understood that he would be reported to the Gestapo. The same day someone tipped my father that the Gestapo was going to investigate our house the next day. We heeded the warning but we never found out who had warned us.

We immediately prepared to get rid of all incriminating evidence. Our neighbors, Mr. Andre Cerf and his family, opened their doors to us, hiding my father's manuscript (remember his "Masterpiece"?) and all the paraphernalia used in printing his weekly letter. Everything went to the Cerfs—ink, paper, primitive press, and stencils. They guarded all this although it could have been very dangerous for them.

— CHAPTER TWENTY-THREE —
The Return of the Gestapo

The fourth of February 1942 will always be imprinted on my mind. It was a sunny but terribly cold day. We went to school as usual, and my father went to work leaving my mother in charge—as usual. My father knew that he was the target of an investigation but never suspected that my mother would have any value to the Gestapo. My brother came home at lunchtime, and since the Gestapo hadn't been to the house yet, my mother asked Guy to stay with her, skipping school that afternoon. She wanted his company to face the Gestapo. Sure enough at 1:00 PM, two trench-coated agents knocked on the door and started their investigation. They were not funny; they were stone faced and efficient in both word and action. The taller one of the two was blond with close-cropped hair and his thin lips looked like a saber slash; his companion was a skinny little runt with a strand of dark hair hanging across his forehead very much like his boss Hitler's.

First they searched my father's office, but to their dismay couldn't find anything. Then they proceeded to go upstairs where they erupted into our apartment screaming in German. They always screamed it seemed to me; I guess it is due to the guttural nature of the language. To us, sick of the occupation and the war, they sounded like sick seals. They took a look around and noticed two small lead soldiers on the mantelpiece, one holding an American flag, the other the Union Jack. That really angered them. They asked my mother who those toy soldiers were (as though they didn't know), but the poor woman was shaking like a leaf, so she let my brother give the explanation. He replied, "Oh, these are our allies, we believe in their victory." They roared angrily, tossing the little soldiers on the floor.

While scanning our living room, they spotted the radio, which they immediately turned on, fumbling with the knobs, hoping to catch us tuned to the BBC. But we knew their tricks, and after hearing the Allied news on the British station we always tuned our radio back to a Belgian station. They then asked to be taken upstairs to our bedrooms. There was not a peep coming from the Heumanns' apartment. Yet I am sure they knew the Gestapo was investigating us. However, let me say one thing in the Gestapo's favor; the agents were thorough in their search but didn't ransack the drawers and closets they were looking in. They also refrained from pocketing our possessions such as jewels and watches. They were interested in finding written texts and weapons.

On the fourth floor they went directly to my and my sister's bedroom, bypassing my brother's bedroom as they had done previously. They just ignored his closed bedroom door. In Europe doors are kept closed at all times. I believe it is on account of different air pressures causing drafts. In winter the reason is loss of heat from one room to another especially in houses that are not centrally heated, and there were many of these.

For the second time our house was searched. Yet my brother's room was left untouched; the closed door by-passed. They searched the spare room—not very thoroughly but never went to the garret, right under the roof, accessible by a ladder.

Once again they came to our apartment and told my mother to put her coat on and accompany them to the Gestapo office for interrogation, suggesting she take some food along for good measure. Guy warned, "Take a good portion mother, they don't feed you well there." The blond and more aggressive Gestapo agent couldn't believe his ears; he turned abruptly around facing my brother with fire in his eyes. Had he been a dragon my brother would have been torched. He yelled in perfect French, "And how do you know that?"

My brother replied truthfully, "Because I have spent time there already." Then the Gestapo told my brother to pack his things because he was going along with my mother.

My poor mother had been feeding the rabbits and had to wash her hands before putting on the thin coat she had been wearing for years now. She felt diminished yet she was young and proud and never hesitated to follow their orders. The agent left a note for my father ordering him to present himself at the Gestapo building as soon as he came home.

My sister and I were at school and had no idea of what was going on at home. When we came home to an empty house, we were anxious, but had no idea that my mother and brother had been taken prisoner. My mother had left us a note asking us to rinse out the few pieces of laundry that she had placed in a bucket to soak and to continue feeding the rabbits because the feeding had been interrupted by the arrival of the Gestapo.

It dawned on us how difficult it had been for my mother to keep the household running with all the restrictions imposed on her and especially to keep us clean without running water because of the frozen pipes. At five o'clock or thereabouts, my father came back from the job he despised and read the note from the Nazi, which by the way was written in perfect French, no spelling error, no syntax mistake. My father took one look at the note and reassured my sister and me that he was going downtown and that they would probably release my mother and brother because he was the culprit. He took some food with him; the only thing available was that ignominious bread with jam. He was certain that *maman* and Guy would be coming home.

— CHAPTER TWENTY-FOUR —

Resourceful Sisters

It was already dark. Days are very short in winter in Belgium and therefore very gloomy, but Ginette and I did not panic. Papa had told us they would be coming back and papa was always right. Time dragged on; still no maman, no Guy. Curfew was on. The last street car for the day had passed by.

To make matters worse the stove started to act up. Neither Ginette nor I had ever built a fire; we had seen papa and my mother light and tend a fire, yet somehow we had only mastered the gestures. When it came to lighting the fire for real we were at a total loss. We still had some kindling, some newspapers, and that terrible *shlam* still dripping wet, which would extinguish the fire as soon as we put it on the brightly burning pieces of wood. I patiently dropped the *schlam* carefully, the way I had seen my parents do, it hissed as it touched the flames and of course smothered them, and the smelly black smoke enveloped us and made our eyes water. Let's start again—empty the stove first, bunch the newspaper, put the kindling on in a criss-cross pattern, light the match, and pray. Put the *schlam* on and pray really hard. Didn't take. And then we realized that we were never going to be warm again and that it was the fault of the heinous Nazis upstairs. I took the poker and started banging it on the marble fireplace and both Ginette and I started to curse the enemy screaming at the top of our lungs. We decided to go to bed, upstairs in our room, as we wanted to keep our routines as normal as possible.

We discussed going to live with our grandparents, but my grandfather was an undertaker and the sight of coffins, black drapes, and hushed tones gave us the creeps; furthermore, we had to stay home and keep an eye on our enemy. We had another grandmother, papa's mother, Yand, as we called her, but my parents and she were not on speaking terms and we hadn't told her that my parents had been arrested.

When my sister and I came downstairs the next morning the water bucket and pitcher bore thin coats of ice; it was that cold in the kitchen. We found out then that we had to start a fire and keep it burning. Thank goodness we had our hour of gas just then and in no time it was warm in the kitchen. We gulped down our breakfast, one slice of bread and that horrible coffee, and off to school we went. No streetcars went directly to my sister's school so she had to walk the proverbial five miles to and from school. We stayed in school for lunch. I was more fortunate: my school was situated in the center of Brussels, served by a tramway for which my parents had purchased my three-month pass.

School at that time started 8:00 AM and I had to take the 7:20 AM tram in order to get to school on time. A tardy arrival meant that the concierge had to unlock the front door. This obliged the student to ring the bell, sign the late book, and wait for the principal to practically kill, first with her looks and then with her mean tongue.

The day after my parents were taken to Saint Gilles Prison I missed my trolley and was late, caught by the principal who told me in no uncertain terms that I was a disgrace to the school and that my dirty nails were not acceptable. I kept silent and didn't tell her about my bout with starting a fire a short time before and that we had very little water with which to wash. I was so terrified of her and her sanctions that I didn't dare tell her my parents had been arrested. She would not have listened to me. We were not permitted to discuss the war situation. We had to remain totally neutral. Her school came first and she was fearful of stepping on the enemy's toes. So she made me scrub my nails and I had to promise never to come to school looking unkempt. I asked her if I could benefit from the free school soup at lunchtime and looking at my thin face she reluctantly acquiesced. My sister, on the other hand, went right away to Mademoiselle Lemaire, her principal, who immediately took steps with the Red Cross to have my sister benefit from whatever was available to her.

That night after school, we went back home and tackled the stove again, but this time we tried to light a fire in the kitchen range because it was the night that we didn't get gas, and we had to cook our dinner. I was more relaxed and this time the kindling and newspaper started to burn, the *schlam* was dry enough to ignite and it worked. Hurrah! We were proud of our achievement so we decided to tell our friends, the Cerfs, how we had managed to do the impossible. They immediately invited us to share their dinner, which was slim pickings. The next night we were invited to have dinner with another neighbor, Mr. Dom, a widower who had two young daughters and a maid. The pickings there were not as slim as at our dear friends the Cerfs.

Mr. Dom lived in a cozy apartment in a modern building. I loved his living room located at the front of the house. Large windows faced the street. Belgians have a passion for big windows, a passion shared by the Dutch. They love that northern exposure and the true light it produces; there is nothing fake about it. Northern light is white and enhances colors, not playing tricks as other lights do. It can be very gloomy in Belgium, known for never ending rain, yet I loved Mr. Dom's place. On cloudy days he used to part the sheer curtains that veiled the windows, but even when the curtains were closed the filtered light was warm and pleasant. Mr. Dom's wife had died quite a number of years before the war and he was left to raise his two little girls. The sad story of his life made the whole family very appealing to my sister and me. We were glad to spend time with him and his two daughters who were younger than we. Mr. Dom was a veteran of WW I and told us his war stories and the tricks he had used to harass the enemy. He was kind enough to share his food with us and courageous enough to invite us to his home. We were *persona non grata* (a person who is not welcome or not wanted) and anybody who was found feeding us was guilty by association. Yet many of our school friends and neighbors invited us to share their meager supplies with us. Afterwards we returned to our cold house ready to struggle with the stoves.

I was still eligible for my bowl of soup at lunchtime. I found out it was sponsored by an organization called "*Secours d'Hiver,*" which translates "Winter Help," a piece of Nazi propaganda; the Nazis were the sponsors of that charity. They were trying to prove to us that they were concerned about the school children's well being. But at least the principal was letting me get the soup, a clear broth with floating vegetables, and before we plunged our spoon in we had to remove the bugs floating on top. At least, it was meat, we rationalized.

That principal was very strict. I could imitate the way she spoke. I had also mastered the way the Flemish teacher talked and had perfected the speech pattern of our lisping history teacher. The Flemish teacher's voice was nasal; I knew she had it in for me for not embracing the Flemish language with fervor; furthermore, she would always catch me for **picayune** infractions. In between classes, to my schoolmates' delight, I used to imitate the three of them having a conversation, and because I was always in trouble I had accumulated an impressive number of expressions used to chastise delinquents such as I. The principal's favorite saying used to be "you are not worthy of this school," and she told me this on many occasions. One day during an unusual long class intermission, the kids asked me to imitate the dynamic trio, which, without too much prodding, I proceeded to do. The kids were roaring and that of course didn't discourage me. Little by little the laughter diminished, and suddenly stopped altogether. I had my back to the door and had not seen that the principal had entered and had been listening to my antics.

My innocent pranks didn't endear me to her heart. A few days after my parents' arrest I was called to her office. A representative of the Belgian Red Cross had contacted the school and had told the principal that my parents were in prison. The Red Cross lady was waiting to talk to me in the anteroom. She was a tall woman, well dressed, who looked at me with sympathy and understanding. I believe she must have noticed the principal's lack of kindness toward me and her lack of involvement in the visitation. The Belgian Red Cross representative had seen my mother who had requested that the Red Cross come to visit me in school. I found out from her that my mother was doing well and thought about us all the time. I cried and couldn't wait to go home and tell my sister. My principal at that juncture forbade me to tell anyone in the school that my parents were political prisoners but she promised the Red Cross representative that I would get the soup *gratis pro Deo* (literally—provided by God; free). When I got back home, I discovered that the same lady had visited my sister but her principal, Mademoiselle Lemaire, had been in touch with people who could help us fend a little better. At least she didn't tell my sister to keep quiet because the more we talked about our problems, the more help was available. My sister also contacted the Savings Bank where my father worked, and although my father was absent, they made an exception so we continued receiving his paycheck every month.

The next morning we had to face the same situation again. The first thing was building the fire in the kitchen. We were in a rush to be ready in order to be at school on time. It was my job to start the fire, an impossible task, until one day I spotted Mr. Dom's cleaning woman coming up the street. I frantically called her to help us with the bloody stove and sure enough with all the right ingredients and a big dose of know-how, the fire burned nicely. The nice woman didn't speak French; she spoke Flemish and looked intently at the uncooperative range, repeating over and over, "It's going to take." When she wasn't available, I would try to duplicate her gestures and repeat her incantations—"it's going to take." "It's going to take" in Flemish, and sure enough that stove would work and we would have warm water to transport to the bathroom so we could wash and keep clean.

We used to come home after school at around 4:30 PM, struggle with the stoves, do our homework, then go to dinner at some friend's house, and be home at around 9:00 PM. We didn't have the key to the house, but since we could not shut the door anymore we always had a way of getting in. The door remained ajar, until one night, when we arrived home and saw that he Heumanns had found a way and the strength to shut the door tight, which would not then yield to our efforts. We were totally unable to open it. We could have rung the Heumanns' doorbell and had them come down and open the door for us but our pride forbade such things. Our alternative was to wait patiently outside until someone from inside the house would come out. The only avenue left to us was to sleep in papa's car parked on the side of the house, slim shelter on that bitter cold night. We had to do it, since we were not allowed out of doors after 10:00 PM and to walk all the way to our grandparents' would have put us in jeopardy. We curled up inside the car on the moldy smelling cushions and slept poorly until dawn. Thank Goodness, Mr. Heumann had to leave for work early the next day, leaving the door ajar, which permitted us to sneak inside our house without their help.

— CHAPTER TWENTY-FIVE —

We Visit St. Gilles

Then one fine day we received a letter from my mother giving us a very few details about her life in jail and urging us to go to the Gestapo and request a pass to visit her in prison. At that time we had no school on Thursday afternoons, which gave us the opportunity to accompany my grandmother to the Gestapo. There we had a meeting with the agent responsible for visitations. My grandmother started to implore the Nazi to give us a pass to see my mother. She was pleading with tears in her eyes and hands joined in prayer, which made me really mad. It hurt me to see my dear grandmother almost kneeling in front of that monster. I harshly told her to stop begging. The German officer yelled at me and threatened to put me in jail "with that snot nosed brother of yours."

I was wearing purple suede gloves, at least two sizes too small. I hated the color but I had to wear them to please my grandmother who had bought them some years before, and I all I was thinking of was to slap that Gestapo guy with them. However, he gave us permission to go to the prison with a pass, duly signed. He also gave us an envelope containing my brother's pass to the opera and the key to his room. We were thrilled to have my brother's ticket to the opera; now we could invite someone to go with us. We were told also that we could bring a small box of food for my mother, one for Guy, and one for papa.

The following Thursday afternoon we took the trolley to the Prison de St. Gilles and sitting right across from me in the trolley was a classmate friend of mine accompanied by her mother who was holding a small package on her lap. That streetcar by the way was loaded with people going to visit political prisoners, so we had a common bond. However, I was stunned to see my friend Jeanne Demeer, and curious I asked, "Who are you visiting?" She told me that her father had been arrested on February 4, but she had been told by our dear principal to keep silent about the arrest. This was the date my parents had been imprisoned. Indeed, her father's cell number was the same as my father's. A few days later it was indeed confirmed by my father in a letter to us that he was in the same cell as Jeanne's father. As before, we could write to my parents and brother once a fortnight but only one page long.

We could also bring a package of food and some money. My brother kept a diary, which he wrote in French using the Greek alphabet. One entry in his journal tells how he had spotted my mother going in a Gestapo car for interrogation, he guessed, and how elated he was at seeing her face again. I was never permitted to visit my brother; that invitation was made to my sister who brought him some goodies given by neighbors of ours. She came back pretty shaken after seeing how skinny he was.

Then one day the Gestapo permitted my sister and me to see our mother. It was quite unnerving to talk to my mother through iron bars. We couldn't touch each other. We cried but not much because we didn't want to show any kind of weakness to the German guard who was eavesdropping on our conversation. Maman 's tone of voice was firm as she tried to build up our courage by exhorting us to be patient, attend school and be kind to our grandparents.

We told her about the kindness and generosity of our friends and we tried to make light of the situation. We knew that we all had a hard time of it, but there was no point in depleting our strength by telling about our mutual trials and tribulations. Believe me, in certain cases it is more difficult to paint a rosy picture than tell the brutal truth. At that session she told us that every night at the same time someone whistled the first bar of "Good night Sweetheart," just that—"good night sweetheart"— and nothing more. She refused to tell us that the food was totally inadequate for fear of depressing us even more. Just to see her made us feel great even if her hair was a mess and she wasn't wearing any make up.

We still had to go to school though, but it became a comfort to me to know my friend Jeanne's father was in the company of my father. Any time we received news from them we could at least share a little something. As a matter of fact, we received a letter from papa and one from my mother. Oh, what a difference in their attitudes and the content of their letters. Papa's was centered upon his terrible condition, the injustice of his incarceration, the abominable food they were given, and how miserable the portions were, plus the fact that he was becoming skeletal, and on and on. Unlike my father, mother didn't talk about herself, but urged us to be brave and gave us directions on how to conduct our lives. We waited for the day my parents would come home but by then the weather started to become more temperate, and the pipes, which had so cruelly frozen, finally thawed out.

— CHAPTER TWENTY-SIX —

Sisters in Charge

The rabbits were doing well although feeding them was a terrible burden on both of us. It was impossible to feed them carrots, too expensive and hard to find. So I was always scavenging for cabbage leaves in the open market, held once a week in the public square in the vicinity of my school. I had to be quick and nimble because I was in competition with others doing the same. After I had filled my school bag with the leaves that were littering the cobblestones I would go home with a smile on my face. I knew that our rabbits would eat something that day.

Once as I began my harvesting on the market square, I was surprised to see lots of leaves still littering the pavement and not a picker to be seen. This kept me wondering. Generally people would fight for those cabbage leaves, yet that day I was picking them up with ease but under the gaze of a crowd that was forming around me. Undaunted, I continued my menial work until one perplexed person asked me, "What are you going to do with these?" My very first impulse was to scoff at that fool's ignorance and keep the secret to myself. Doing something unusual and out of place, such as picking dead cabbage leaves by a nice little girl, provoked a lot of suspicion from the spectators who were always eager to discover a new use for something that before the war was never used. I was experiencing a feeling of elation comparable to the one James Marshall, the guy who found the first gold nugget at Sutter Mill must have felt. I played it cool. I was smug. Then I looked up at the crowd with contempt painted on my face and replied in a superior tone of voice: "What do you think I am going to do with cabbage leaves when I have rabbits to feed?" Some kind soul told me in a tone of relief, "Kid, these are rhubarb leaves; they will kill your rabbits; they are poisonous; nobody wants them." Then someone else told me in no uncertain terms: "And keep them in your school bag. Because if you dare to put those leaves back on the ground, I'll give you a citation followed by a ticket." I was therefore condemned to take my streetcar ride home with a schoolbag chockfull of garbage under the mocking gaze of the fools I had snubbed a few minutes before.

My school was located in the middle of Brussels in one of the poorest districts also known as *les Marolles*, and I still can picture children sick with rickets, being pushed in special carriages around town. Those children were terribly pale and their legs were so skinny that it was impossible for them to stand on them, let alone walk; wearing white long stockings, they were lying down stretched on special baby carriages. This gave me an eerie feeling, one of being transported back to the Middle Ages. Yet these children had been malnourished since birth and their defects were not a result of the privation due to wartime. The whole atmosphere of "Old Brussels" gave me an eerie feeling. Picture the medieval buildings with stone facades delicately chiseled resembling fine lace, the narrow and winding streets, the sick children, the street vendors wearing heavy garments and wooden shoes; these all lent an air of the medieval to the former bustling atmosphere of my beloved Brussels. And now carts being pulled by horses were replacing automobiles lending a circus-y-like smell to our surroundings.

— CHAPTER TWENTY-SEVEN —

Many Questions

M y sister and I felt very close then. We were fighting the unknown—all alone—and that gave us a feeling of strength and independence. We were able to survive without our parents' supervision and that taught us to be careful and frugal. I don't remember being scared. Angry? Yes. Frustrated? Oh my, furious even, but not scared. I was seventeen; my sister, fourteen. We were "Captains of our souls, Masters of our destiny." And best of all we had my brother's pass to the opera. The opera being played the day stipulated on our pass was *Faust,* the magical Berlioz's opera, which I loved for the music and the scenery and the vintage 1940s special effects: flowers that lighted up when Marguerite touched them, Mephistopheles squirming in holy water during the church segment of the play, the fantastic ballet, the contract signed between the Devil and Dr. Faust, and finally the ascension of Marguerite into Heaven. My mother had not told us about the birds and the bees yet. I hadn't read the libretto and had ignored that poor Marguerite was pregnant, expecting Dr. Faustus' baby, and had died in childbirth.

I should have suspected something when the devil was involved. I went to listen to the music, which I loved, but somehow my mind was not at ease. I was on pins and needles. I had promised Guy's ticket to my friend Jeanne to cheer her up, and my sister had promised the same ticket to her friend Sheila. We were worried, hoping that one of them wouldn't show up. They were there at the appointed time so we had to sneak one of them in and show the same ticket twice, which we accomplished easily. Belgians are great at doing magic tricks and using sleight of hand when necessary. However, the theater was packed and if we had entered easily and hoodwinked the ticket man at the gate, the usherette was not that easily fooled. "One butt per seat" was her motto, and she could see that there were more butts than seats available. I was in a panic, but my sister who was the level headed one told me to cool it; she had investigated the situation and had slipped two francs to the usher to keep her quiet and find us an unoccupied seat. We returned home happy and content.

Ginette and I went to the movies too. We saw a French movie with Danielle Darieux and I believe that at that time we even saw a movie with Deana Durbin and Leopold Stokowski about a young girl and one hundred musicians (*One Hundred Men and a Girl*, 1937). The film was so romantic that it should have inspired us to romance, yet we were so hungry, pale, and skinny that we didn't even think about romance. Our main objective was to stay alive until after the war. We were also very immature, and the more mature had the decency to respect us and avoided putting us in a defensive position. Life although tough had some great moments, creating a profound bond between us. This bond gave us much confidence and love.

My sister and I were just about to start our spring planting after having fertilized the ground with the rabbits' droppings, which we cleaned from the cages every so often, when we discovered that the rabbits had a way to communicate with one another. We had six rabbits, six hutches, and one rabbit to each hutch. When we fed them they seemed to be in their places, one per cage, until one day we discovered an unusual amount of fur in one corner of one cage—loose white hair, cotton ball stuff. After our eyes adjusted to the dim light of the courtyard, we saw a slew of baby bunnies. Unfortunately they were not all alive and well. Our neighbor told us afterwards that a female becomes thirsty after the birth of the babies and finds relief in drinking her progeny's blood, thereby killing them. He also explained to me that the rabbits had squeezed their little bodies between the partitions in order to satisfy their need to populate the earth with many, many bunnies. That put a damper on my love for those furry creatures; they looked so innocent in their little cages and yet at night they were having sex. I thought they were a bunch of hypocrites, chewing so peacefully and yet hoodwinking us into believing they were virginal and doing God knows what when our backs were turned.

I guess that the bad behavior of those rabbits prompted my neighbor to take on my parents' job—telling me a thing or two about the birds and the bees and in this case the bunnies. He was flabbergasted by my innocence and my lack of knowledge about sex. Since he used euphemisms to name the parts of the body that were unfamiliar to me, it still didn't make any sense to me, and I remained in a fog even after his very sketchy explanations. Furthermore, I didn't believe him.

— CHAPTER TWENTY-EIGHT —

The Family Together

Before we had time to organize the planting details, one afternoon in July 1942, when we came home from school, my parents and brother were home. I still remember our joy knowing that we were together again. My parents looked terrible, especially my father who looked haggard and emaciated. My mother's cheeks were hollow which made her teeth look as though they were protruding, but she was so happy to be home again that she didn't care how they looked. We hugged each other, and my brother once again became our hero.

However, our tenant, Mr. Heumann, upon his return from work became enraged when he found out that my parents and brother had been released from jail. He exploded with rage, trying to harm my father by running after him with a broken bottle. Thank God, my father had the presence of mind to run toward the cellar locking the door behind him, leaving Mr. Heumann gesturing like a maniac and ranting like an insane animal. My brother went immediately to the Belgian police who came to try to pacify my father's attacker. Since it was a civilian feud involving a German citizen, the matter was turned over to the *Politzei* who gave orders to Heumann to vacate the premises and try to find other lodgings. The next day the family moved out of the apartment but remained in Brussels, as we found out later on.

My parents were in pitiful health; while being interrogated in prison, a Gestapo had kicked my father in the shin and that wound had become infected. Because of my father's sorry state of health and the lack of medicines available, life became hard especially on my mother. Papa was not a combative sick person. No, papa was not your Spartan. He remained bedridden for a while but resumed his activities reluctantly after his leg showed improvement. He returned to his office where his coworkers greeted him effusively. Upstairs, the apartment was vacant, which turned out to be a great thing.

While in prison my brother had kept a journal, written on toilet paper, and to add a clever twist he had used the Greek alphabet in order to confuse his captors and his fellow inmates. Later on he faithfully transcribed the whole thing in a copybook, using the same symbols. After many years, I started to transcribe my brother's notes into our own script since I was fortunate enough to be able to read the Cyrillic letters (one of the scripts invented to write Slavic letters, derived from Greek—ancientscripts.com). I couldn't wait to translate my brother's thoughts and be part of the ordeal he had to endure at the hands of the enemy. It is only lately that I have found the time and courage to tackle his writings, which could be labeled as chicken scratch.

Because they were written in phonetic French I drained my energy trying to decipher Guy's poor little journals. What a surprise! The diary told mostly of what he had to eat. He described not only the number of portions he received every day but approximately their size and color. I found out that he had placed a few requests to see General von Falkenhauser, who was in charge of the prison and an important official among the Germans. He seemed to be appalled at my brother's condition and responded, ordering my brother to receive a special ration of cod liver oil. He happened to have a son my brother's age so he showed compassion for Guy. He also shook his head at my brother's impudence but overall was very decent to my infamous *frère*. Guy happened to be the youngest person incarcerated in the jail. As I studied the journal, I was looking for some juicy spy stories, cloak and dagger stuff, and then I remembered that my brother was only fifteen years old and that food was the primary concern of kids that age.

Guy also wrote about his cellmates one of whom had been incarcerated for dealing in foreign currency. His name was Yves Shaffir. My brother related that on a certain day Shaffir had been called to report to the Gestapo building where he was driven in an armored car. It was a terrible blow to his cellmates who feared the

worst. Yves Shaffir was Jewish, and they expected that he had
been sent away to Germany. Afterwards they learned their friend
had been transferred to another prison, one reserved for common
criminals, and released after serving his sentence. He had become
indispensable to the Germans thanks to his connections with
foreign banks and trafficking dollars. Thus he escaped being sent
to a concentration camp.

— CHAPTER TWENTY-NINE —

Hiding Jews

As soon as the Heumanns left, my father put the apartment
up for rent and kind of forgot to tell the authorities that
there was a vacant apartment in our house. It was
compulsory to tell the authorities that there was a vacancy;
however, my father did not want Germans occupying the place, so
he didn't bother to make a formal declaration. It didn't take long
to find new tenants who were delighted to occupy the spacious
quarters. It was rented to a young couple and their little daughter,
Martha. Mr. Schipper, who had been a diamond merchant in
Antwerp, had decided to move to Brussels.

His wife was a vivacious brunette with abundant hair pulled
back severely into a bun. Her hair must have been very long since
the bun was huge, shiny and the color of ripe chestnuts. I
remember her dancing eyes and her devilish smile. She
immediately took to my sister and vice versa. They became fast
friends and my sister was delighted to baby-sit little Martha in
return for Mrs. Schipper's affection. We liked her too because she
had a quick sense of humor and was full of life, a sharp contrast to
her husband who was morose and very reserved. She used to tease
him in a kind way and his patience knew no bounds.

There had been rumors that the Germans were rounding up
Jewish people. This was another reason my father refused to tell the
authorities about the vacant apartment; it could become very handy
later on. We had also found out that our new tenants were Jewish.

Little by little, things started to change. In 1942, the Nazis decreed that all Jews had to wear the Star of David on their lapels. The star was stamped on a piece of yellow cloth and then sewn to every outer garment. This was something of a revelation to us. People that we had known for years all of a sudden had to advertise the fact that they were different from us. For us they were Belgians, and we refused to take a religion as a basis for discrimination. Furthermore, our Jewish friends had to go to City Hall and have the word *JUIF* stamped on their identification cards.

In Europe everybody had to carry a valid and legal document, stating name, address, date of birth, and marital status—the whole thing reinforced by a recent picture. That document had to be carried at all times and was issued to every citizen upon his or her sixteenth birthday. Teenagers couldn't wait to be issued this card that, in fact, infringed upon their freedom. (Ask any United States citizen, who before September 11, 2001, would not have dreamed of carrying a government issued obligatory document. I guess it is a controversial subject.)

At City Hall, the employees were very uncooperative with the German dictates, so instead of using strength and much ink when applying the stamp, they just kissed the card and the word JUIF was barely visible. They discovered that by exposing the document to the sunlight, the word would fade completely away. This was a good thing.

This new regulation forced our tenants to stay indoors and not dare to venture outside. They became totally dependent on us for shopping, taking care of their laundry, and the million little things that normal life requires. Taking care of the little girl became my sister's endeavor. Ginette would take her out in the carriage, but after a while even that became dangerous because the little one looked stereotypically Jewish with black hair and black eyes.

Mr. Schipper used to come down to our apartment to listen to the BBC at 5:00 PM every day. The news bulletins at that time were given in Polish and were not garbled by the Nazis. Since our tenant could understand Polish it was rather nice for us to be privy to first hand news. However, the poor man was scared to death to be caught by our neighbors, who lived 500 meters from our house and who could denounce to the Gestapo. He was afraid to arouse the suspicion of the neighbors since he was glued to that radio at the same time every day. Old radios dials were feebly lighted and Mr. Schipper was afraid that the neighbors would be able to detect that light every day at 5 :00 PM. I want to say that the amperage and wattage of the light couldn't even be measured in lumens; however, he requested my father to draw the drapes each time he listened to the news. It didn't make sense to me. Wouldn't the neighbors find it suspicious that our curtains were drawn at the same time every day? After I gave him my bit of logic, he decided to change his modus operandi (a person's way of working).

One day my father discovered a hole in the guestroom ceiling but after an investigation and accusing us of having been careless, Mr. Schipper confessed to my father that he had hidden a small pouch of diamonds, his earthly possessions, in the attic but had inadvertently missed the rafter and almost fell through the plaster ceiling of the guestroom. Mr. Schipper would go to the attic and retrieve diamonds that he would sell to the black market through the help of some friends, notably Sylvia, a spinster, whose sister would sometimes stay with the Schippers with her little boy Louis. Mr. Schipper relied on some other Jewish friends who used to come to our house to help him sell the diamonds, but after a while that became too dangerous.

When the situation became dangerous, he called on Ginette to help him unload his precious cargo, without giving her any details. My father knew about it but refrained from telling my sister what it was all about. They figured that if she knew what the small bag contained she would be unable to conceal her fear and remain poker faced. As far as the hole in the ceiling we had to leave it the way it was since having someone repair it could arouse suspicion. We were now formally hiding Jews in that undeclared apartment and we had to be careful as to whom we would let in the house. Mrs. Schipper was especially distraught to be stuck in that apartment and lived vicariously through my sister. Madame Schipper had very good taste and used to wear stylish clothes. She and Ginette were the same size, so Madame Schipper would loan Ginette a great looking jacket when she had to attend a special occasion and even told my sister that at least the jacket had permission to have a good time.

From Arlette's *carnet de poesies* (scrap book of drawings and writings) 1941. These pages were done by Arlette's classmates to show their resistance to the occupation.

Ginette and Arlette just before parents' imprisonment and Guy's second imprisonment.

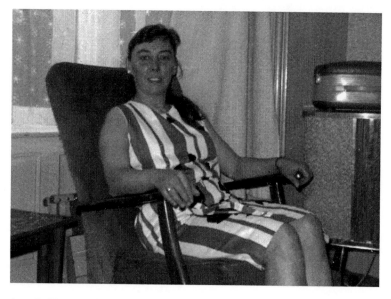

Angele Van Lierde: Angele, who was very active in the underground, was the liaison between Jews and Arlette's father.

To Guy in Saint Gilles Prison (the first time).

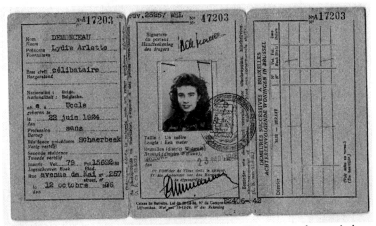

Identification Card—required of all Belgium Citizens, to be carried
at all times.

Ville de Bruxelles

PROCLAMATION

Mes Chers Concitoyens,

L'Autorité allemande vient de me faire savoir que je dois cesser d'exercer mes fonctions de bourgmestre; je ne puis que m'incliner devant cet ordre, quoiqu'en droit il viole la Convention de La Haye et qu'en fait rien ne justifie la mesure prise à mon égard; j'ai en effet conscience d'avoir loyalement et totalement accompli les multiples devoirs toujours lourds et pénibles incombant aux chefs des villes et communes occupées par l'ennemi.

Il m'avait été proposé de continuer l'exercice de mes fonctions, mais dans des conditions telles qu'elles impliquaient de ma part une participation à l'exécution des Arrêtés des 16 avril et 26 mai 1941, pris, par une autorité belge, en violation de la loi du 10 mai 1940 sur laquelle cette même autorité s'appuie pour exercer le pouvoir; en me soumettant, je foulais aux pieds l'honneur et le devoir et je désobéissais à une des lois fondamentales de notre Pays, lois auxquelles j'ai juré obéissance : j'ai refusé.

Contrairement à ce qui se dit, je n'ai pas quitté mon poste et n'ai pas offert ma démission.

JE SUIS, JE RESTE ET JE RESTERAI LE SEUL BOURGMESTRE LÉGITIME DE BRUXELLES.

Tout ce qu'une autorité belge fait et fera en application des susdits arrêtés est sans fondement légal.

Je ne vous fais donc pas mes adieux : je vous dis au revoir.

En vous quittant provisoirement je vous demande de supporter vos misères et vos souffrances matérielles et morales avec CALME, COURAGE, et CONFIANCE ; vous ferez front contre le sort, d'une âme fière et d'un cœur fort.

Ceux qui sont vraiment de notre race n'ont peur de rien ni de personne dans ce monde; ils n'ont qu'une crainte : celle de ne pas faire tout leur devoir et de perdre l'honneur.

Restez unis : votre UNION fera votre FORCE et vous assurera un avenir meilleur !

« Dieu saura protéger la Belgique »
« Et Son Roi »

Le Bourgmestre,
Dᵣ F. J. VAN DE MEULEBROECK.

Hôtel de Ville, 30 juin 1941.

1274. — Imprimerie E. GUYOT, s. a., rue Pachéco, Bruxelles (Dʳ Gʳ A. Posters, 194, rue Edith Cavell, Uccle).

On June 30, 1941, there was a commotion in Brussels. Everybody rushed outside to read a proclamation posted by our beloved Mayor. It was plastered, or rather glued, on every blank wall of the city. (Translation on page 39.)

Arlette and Guy: taken just before Guy's second imprisonment in 1941

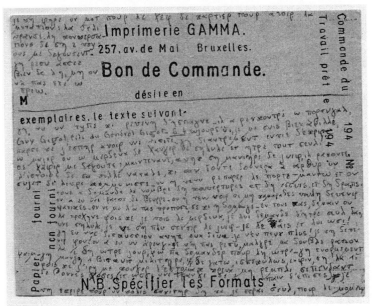

Page of the diary Guy kept in St. Gilles Prison written in French using the ancient Greek alphabet.

Arlette and two children hidden by Father Bruno, Tammy and Moses Englander (8 and 9 years), two orphans, who are to be adopted by Maurice Schwartz, director and actor. Photo first published in a Belgian newspaper at the time—1947.

Cathy (Philippe's wife), Philippe, Arlette, and Leslie (Arlette's daughter)—atop Old England Building in Brussels, Belgium, October 2003.

— CHAPTER THIRTY —

The Cerfs

Our dear friends, the Cerfs, who had helped my sister and me while my parents were incarcerated and had kept our incriminating evidence at their house, surprised us one day by wearing the yellow star We had no idea they were Jewish and we urged them not to wear it. They realized very quickly that it made them vulnerable when the Nazis decided to make an impromptu raid and close a street at both ends. They would block both ends of a street and verify identification papers. Whoever looked suspicious or was a Jew not wearing the yellow star would be escorted to a military truck and driven away. Monsieur Cerf had been a major in the Belgian army and considered himself invulnerable. Unfortunately the Gestapo thought otherwise.

One afternoon, as Madame Cerf was coming down our street, she spotted a Gestapo car parked in front of her house and saw her mother opening the downstairs window and surreptitiously setting the key on the outside windowsill. A few minutes later, Madame Cerf witnessed her husband, son, and mother being taken away in a Gestapo car. She never stopped but continued walking straight ahead on legs she described later as being made of soft rubber. She never gave a hint to the captors that it was her family they were taking away. Neighbors who had witnessed her courageous action immediately invited her to stay with them.

She was not permitted to enter her house because the Gestapo had placed seals on the front door but she retrieved the key her mother had placed on the windowsill. The seals did not deter my friend, Madame Cerf. The next day she marched to City Hall and told one of the employees that her family had been taken by the Gestapo and her home sealed. She demanded to be let into her house. She was told that it was a Gestapo matter. However, if she needed protection to enter her home, they would be willing to help and keep watch while she cut the seals placed on the front door. They suggested her going at dusk, promising they would be there. And sure enough at the appointed time, Madame Cerf, surrounded by her newfound friends from City Hall, entered her home and started collecting her precious belonging under the watchful eyes of her buddies. She put all her treasures in a bed sheet she had spread on the living room floor, tied the whole thing *a la hobo*, and flung the package over the wall into her neighbor's garden. She realized days after the shock that in her hurry she had put into her bed sheet a bunch of unnecessary things, such as silver candlesticks and napkin rings.

She spent the first horrendous night at a neighbor's and the next day marched heroically not to the Gestapo but to the *Kommandantur*, which was the military force occupying Brussels, demanding to speak to the *Kommandant*, who I believe was General Von Falkenhausen, the same General who had prescribed cod liver oil for my brother when he was in prison. Madame Cerf explained to the general that her husband had been a major in the Belgian army and deserved to be treated with respect. Curiously enough the general listened attentively to her plea; then he told her that he would do his best but could not promise her anything. She was very surprised by the attention she was given by that general, returning to her neighbor's home in high spirits. I have to add that Madame Cerf, a very tall woman, who spoke with an Alsatian accent (an inhabitant of Alsace, a French region, located in the east of France, on the German and Swiss border), was firm in her demeanor, and you could detect that she was a no nonsense person. She was incredibly kind and generous and never hesitated to help friends in need.

A few days later for no apparent reason Mr. Cerf, as well as their son, was released from jail. The son, upon hearing that he was free, ran all the way home (about fifteen miles) not wanting to risk his new found freedom by taking a streetcar. As for the elderly mother, she had been placed in an old folks home with Jewish women who spoke Yiddish, which she could not understand. After all she was French, a proud Alsatian, also a dear soul. She also was freed. To this day the family still wonders why the Gestapo never bothered them again. In the meantime there was no guarantee the *Gestapo* would not return and they lived in fear until the end of the war. You never knew with the Nazis. The Cerfs believed that General Von Falkenhausen extended military

courtesy to a Belgian major even though he was Jewish. Some
people speculated that King Leopold had intervened in Major
Cerf's behalf. Who knows? As I said before, we will never know.

— CHAPTER THIRTY-ONE —

More Suffering for the Jews

Finally in 1943, Jewish children were denied educations,
forbidden to attend public schools. Therefore, the public
and private (Catholic) schools decided to work together so
the Jewish children could stay in school. The Catholic private
schools enrolled the students in name only; that is, they put their
names on their rosters but let the children attend classes at their
regular public schools. The Germans didn't bother private
schools, which they considered unofficial. So the Nazis never
found out about that little ruse and the kids attended school until
it became too dangerous for them to leave their houses. We urged
our Jewish friends, the Isaacs, to stay put and not venture outside,
but they didn't feel targeted since none of them followed the
religion nor attended a synagogue.

My father's friend who had been working with him as an
engineer before the war was certain that he was in no danger
although his last name was Isaac.

He refused to listen to my father. We found out later that the
Gestapo had taken him and his family. That is all we ever heard
about them after they were taken. The same happened to our
friend Jorgen. He was another character, a great friend of my
father's, who unfortunately for him looked "Jewish"; he looked
like pictures of the biblical Abraham. He was the owner of an
electrical manufacturing firm; he rode around Brussels in a little
contraption of his own making—a three-wheeled bike protected
by a small canopy and canvas sides with plastic windows. His
nervous little legs activated this and he could be seen pedaling his
little car over a big portion of Brussels. He was fascinating to me
because he spoke Esperanto (Esperanto is an invented

[constructed] language intended for use between people who speak different languages), which he wanted to teach me, but especially because he told us of his wooing his bride in that language. His wife was young and very pretty, and she adored her Jorgen. As the situation became more and more tense in Brussels, my father counseled Jorgen to go into hiding, if not for his own sake then for his young wife's. Jorgen was not that easily convinced. He could not see the danger. Furthermore, he attracted a lot of attention riding his contraption, which was the only one of its kind not only in Brussels, but also probably in the world. Eventually, as we feared, he and his sweet wife disappeared—never seen nor heard from again. We figured that they had been taken by the Nazis. I was angry at Jorgen for not heeding my father's advice and condemning himself and his wife to death in a concentration camp.

This hurt us very badly. Each time we lost a friend it felt as though someone hit us in the gut. We felt powerless, angry, revengeful, and desperately sad at the same time. The pain made us yell silently inside and it tore at our bellies. Poor Mr. and Mrs. Jorgen.

As the Germans started to lose key positions and to suffer losses in Russia, they became especially cruel toward the Jews and other rebels. They would catch people in the middle of the night, seize them and send them to places that we could not have imagined. At the time we had no idea where they were sent. They were spirited away under the cover of darkness, very quickly and very quietly. Several hours later we would find out that our friends had disappeared. We heard a terrible tale of a young mother who was seized by the Gestapo in the middle of the night and was forbidden to take her baby with her. But before leaving the apartment she turned on the water in the stopped up kitchen sink letting the overflow drip into the apartment below. In order to repair the damage caused by the overflow, the owner of the building had permission to break the seals and enter the premises. Needless to say the landlord, who refused to tell the authorities, immediately rescued the baby.

— CHAPTER THIRTY-TWO —

Father Bruno

Then there was Romek who had been arrested by the Gestapo and put in one of those horrible cattle trains bound for a concentration camp in Germany. He had the guts to sneak out through a tiny window while the train was moving, but as he made his escape was shot in the back. He hid in fields and woods for hours before he could get the medical attention his wound required. The rifle bullet had pierced a lung. By the time he had finally reached a Belgian farm, he could barely breathe. A doctor, who was summoned, attended to his injury, which required hospitalization. That was dangerous because all casualties had to be reported to the Nazis. But the physicians in many cases were faithful to their oath and human life came first.

However, after his release from the hospital, poor Romek had to find lodgings. He knew a wonderful woman, Sonia, a Russian immigrant who spoke with a delightful accent. She had been hiding in Louvain, a town known throughout the world for a Catholic university of great renown. Sonia occupied an apartment belonging to a certain Mrs. Nordens. This apartment had been rented to students before the war. Sonia now shared the apartment with her mother, and she opened her door to Romek. Sonia was older than Romek, and when they decided to marry, the mother was in a panic. Marriage in the neighborhood synagogue was out of the question. However, since they were living in proximity to many, many Catholic churches and under the protection of Father Henri Reynders (Père Bruno) there was no shortage of priests willing to bless their union.

They lived in a room that served as living and dining room alike. However, it was very big, airy, and pleasant, and I had good feelings when I visited them. My friends were kind and full of hope and Sonia would sing those nostalgic and tragic Russian songs in her beautiful voice. I think it was her voice that had attracted Romek.

At that time in Brussels, students had Thursday afternoons off but had to attend school all day on Saturdays. I decided right there and then that I would spend my Thursday afternoons in Louvain with my friends to help them do their shopping or take them to the doctor or whatever errand they had to do which required my protection. Louvain was about one hour away from Brussels by special streetcar and I would forget about my homework in order to help my friends.

Once there, I had to contact a certain Father Bruno Reynders through one of his messengers, a young man by the name of Jean Gregoire. Father Bruno was a Benedictine Monk and was able to provide my Jewish friends with false identification papers, food stamps, money, and rent for their lodging.[10] The owner of the building was a widow who took an instant dislike to me because her son didn't find me repulsive. That young man, Loulou, had been a law student before the war, but now he was mainly involved in underground activities. As a matter of fact, he would pick me up at home and help me carry suitcases full of supplies for Sonia and her gang and even sometimes pay for my tram fare. I think my parents shared the same feelings toward Loulou as his mother felt for me.

I also contacted other Jews, notably one man who had been a fine tailor before the war. As it happened he was in need of medical attention, requiring an operation immediately. Father Bruno Reynders took all the necessary steps required for that man to enter the hospital where he was taken without delay. A few days later he recovered from his operation, returning to his hiding place and his then pregnant wife.

Pregnancies were another difficult situation that required vigilance and immense secrecy in case of complications. At that time many babies were delivered by midwives at home, but we had to find reliable people who would not denounce their patients to the Nazis. Thank God, once again the priests came to the rescue—finding a trustworthy midwife and keeping records of the birth. Father Bruno Reynders, who was instrumental in saving many lives, had a profound respect for freedom of religious convictions and never took the liberty of converting any of his charges to Catholicism. As a matter of fact he emphasized that religious education as well as physical and moral education is a right of the parents.

At home we were still hiding the young couple and their little girl, but things were becoming very scary for us. Mr. Schipper brought some other Jewish refugees to the house and they too were now hiding in our house. Nighttime was a tough time and the sounds of cars made our Jewish tenants very uncomfortable. For only the Gestapo were allowed to drive at night; therefore, any motor noise heard outside used to send them into a panic.

However, there was a possible remedy to the problem. The Gestapo always bypassed my brother's room when they searched my house. They never noticed the door to that room but went directly into my sister's and my bedroom. Therefore, papa asked my grandfather to build a false bookcase hinged to the wall, hiding the door to my brother's room. If in the middle of the night we heard motor sounds and brake noises, our friends just walked up to my brother's bedroom, swung open the phony bookcase, and hid in my brother's bedroom. They would stay there until the danger passed.

Unfortunately, little Martha became a liability. Being awakened from a sound sleep and spirited away into the hideout made the poor little girl cry. Her cries might betray her family to the Gestapo, so her parents were faced with a terrible decision. They decided that their little girl would be better off living on a farm in the country. Our friend from the underground had advised us that some farmers would welcome small children and give them asylum on their farms. It was heartbreaking for the mother to trust the life of her child to strangers, but it had to be done.

We decided to find two farms in the same vicinity that would accommodate the father and the mother and close by a farm where little Martha could find safe haven. It became my father's responsibility to spirit away Mr. Schipper who was literally paralyzed with fear. Mr. Schipper looked Jewish; therefore, we had to find a way to camouflage his appearance. Papa suggested wrapping his head in bandages, giving him the appearance of a war victim, a plausible state of affairs during a war. It was agreed that he would go bandaged like a mummy from the neck up. However, his eyes looked so frightened that my father decided to hide them behind sunglasses, telling him that his eyes would be a dead give away.

There was a fellow by the name of Jacques working for the Gestapo whose job was to point out Jews walking around and not wearing the Star of David on their garments. He had a knack for discovering who was Jewish and was much feared by our little group. It didn't take long to convince Mr. Schipper to disguise himself and accompany my father on the train from Brussels to our friends' farm. My grandparents' friends offered to shelter the little family for a short time, and later on my sister took Martha to the town of Spa.

Spa, a small but charming town, was known for baths and natural mineral water with numerous therapeutic benefits.[11] The hotels in that town were elegant and enjoyed a great reputation. However, during the war, the town's hotels had become rehabilitation sites for mutilated German soldiers. Most of them were missing a leg or two, hobbling on crutches. My sister was surprised to see the multitude of wounded men and remarked this to a nurse who replied that they were nicknamed the "grasshoppers."

Martha was placed with a nice family and my sister now tried to find farmers willing to harbor the parents. After many tries we were able to find a farmer who was trustworthy and Ginette escorted the parents to that farm, located in the vicinity of their daughter's, but they were asked to stay away from the child. It would have been too traumatic for either party to be separated after each visit. The good part was that the mother could watch her little girl from a distance, although that was almost as bad as not being able to see her. The temptation to hold her child and hug her was sometimes worse than being totally separated from the child; it really was torture for the poor mother.

— CHAPTER THIRTY-THREE —

More Renters, More Resistance

Once again the apartment became vacant, and as before my father did not bother declaring this to the German authorities. The apartment became an ideal hiding place for Jews who were now being hunted down unmercifully by the Germans. My friend Angele was the underground mole, the go between the *Maquis* and our house. She introduced us to Mr. and Mrs. Vansteen. They were elderly and had owned a prosperous slipper factory in Amsterdam. They intended to stay with us for only a short time until they could find a more secure place to hide. The Vansteens were very wealthy but frugal, which we understood since we didn't know how long the war was going to last.

Then a fantastic event hit the capital having to do with the newspaper *Le Soir*. The day after our defeat and the king's abdication, the Nazis had seized the Belgian media. Both newspapers, the French and the Flemish editions, were immediately taken over and became media for German propaganda. The same procedure was used to control the airwaves, which became the mouthpiece of the regime. My parents objected to both; we did not listen to the radio any more, and the newspaper only entered our house when donated by the neighbors as toilet paper.

Generally speaking the citizens reading the newspapers were not judged as unpatriotic because for many it had been their custom to read the papers after a long day's work. There was only one edition per day and these newspapers were delivered every day at around four o'clock to the various newsstands around the city.

On November 3, 1943, deliveries were made at the usual time, but when the regular readers began reading they were suddenly shocked at the content. Instead of German propaganda the papers were full of articles urging the Belgians to have faith and persevere because the allied victory was near. The newspaper also explained that the newspaper had been published on Armistice Day,

November 11, and then exhorted the Belgians to remain faithful to their nation. The paper also included a few barbs directed at Adolf Hitler and cartoons that made fun of the Nazis. A few seconds after the patriotic issue was delivered the Nazi propaganda edition of Le Soir hit the kiosks. There was great confusion, aided by the vendors who had initially ignored the subterfuge.

The lucky readers brandished their newspapers believing in a miracle. Everybody was everybody's friend, talking and laughing about the newspaper. There was an air of elation that elevated every spirit. Strangers were talking to strangers, not bothering to hide their hatred for the enemy. Oh what a day! A delightful moment was shared by all! To this day we wonder how it was possible to duplicate the newspaper.

We found out later that some unbelievably audacious members of the underground had published a patriotic newspaper using the same banner as the real one, making their delivery to the newsstand one second before the regular Nazi controlled edition was to be distributed. It didn't take long for the citizens of Brussels to realize what was happening. They rushed to the newsstand hoping to buy the false *Le Soir*, but by that time unfortunately all had disappeared. The patriots, who had published the false *Soir*, as it came to be known, were never caught and some more editions were published and sold to benefit the underground. They were sold at five francs a copy instead of fifty centimes, the regular cost, and the proceeds were given to wives and children of political prisoners. Papa and my sister became distributors and received substantial contributions from people who were willing to pay a lot more than five francs for such a precious piece of memorabilia. Even our Dutch slipper makers, the Vansteens, bought a copy for five francs.

At this time the war in Russia was ravaging the German army. We heard that Mr. Heumann had been called into the army and was fighting on the Russian front. Every night we rejoiced at their defeats. First the Germans and then the Russians had captured Stalingrad in the Soviet Union (Battle of Stalingrad June 28, 1942-February 2, 1943). The city of Perekop, also in the Soviet Union, was next to be taken and retaken (1944), and we heard of the number of casualties suffered by both sides. But as the Nazis lost on the Russian Front, they became more and more vicious and would punish any infraction we would commit.

It became dangerous for the Vansteens to stay with us any longer, so they decided to find a safer place and asked if we could take in their niece, Carrie, the niece's fiancé, Freddy, and their nephew Leo. However, when Uncle and Aunt Vansteen found out that Carrie and Freddy were living in the same apartment, they were shocked, deciding to cut their allowances. The poor young people were frantic.

Leo, Carrie, and Freddy were in their twenties, so Ginette and I became their great friends. We didn't want them to go away. They spoke both French and Dutch and every night they would come down to our apartment where we shared great moments together. They would help us with Dutch, which is a refined Flemish, and we would teach them French. Carrie was especially nice and intelligent, possessing a fantastic sense of humor as did her fiancé, a good-looking lad. Leo was the reasonable one and I used to accompany him when he had to do errands for the family. I remember accompanying him to Antwerp on several occasions and I was proud to be that fine looking young man's date. Leo was very tall, wore rimless glasses and his black hair gave the impression that his smooth hair had been painted on his head.

But the best part of our time together was the time we spent with their cousin who came for a visit once in a while. His name was also Leo, but since he was shorter than his cousin, he became known as "Little Leo" or in Dutch, *Leotje*. He was a musician and his guitar rendition of "Miss Otis regrets..." was superb. We all spoke English when our French or Dutch became garbled, and we talked about a rosy and wonderful future. Not only was Leotje an artist, he was kind and gentle with a great sense of humor. He wrote some memorable stuff in my autograph book. He had a crush on my friend Angele and they became engaged for a while. Leotje became the liaison between Carrie and the aunt and uncle and so a pact was made with the old people. Then the old people were happy and resumed sending the young ones their most deserved allowance.

Although we were living in uncertain times we had bonded and relished every minute we spent together. Strangely enough we could find fun things to say and do with all the **élan** that our age permitted. During all that time I was still going to Louvain to support and help my friends Sonia and Romek and Sonia's mother. Then I heard terrible news about my friend Jean Gregoire. He had been spotted by someone, not for being Jewish but for helping Father Bruno, and was sent to Germany. I was devastated because he was very dear not only to me but also to my friends. With his arrest I lost contact with the underground because I had no way to get in touch with Father Bruno. I had to be very careful and tried to be as circumspect as possible.

Many Jewish children had to be hidden in safe places and we had found out that convents were an ideal place to hide and educate children. My father posed as their father and lent his name to a slew of little kids who were hidden in a convent in Bruges. My sister and I took turns accompanying the children to the forbidding confines of the convent. What a dreary place.

Bruges (Flemish—*Brugge*) is an ancient place yet delightful for art and history connoisseurs, but for little kids it was smelly, old, and rather scary. Of course there is a magnetic charm associated with the place but in 1944 Bruges was a mess. The once romantic canals hadn't been taken care of and were incredibly polluted. The swans that once graced the canals had died because of the pollution and a definite smell permeated that town.

Bruges now has been totally rehabilitated and once again the swans are floating with peace and grace on the very clear water of the canals and once again it has become the great cultural center it had been in the past.

At the end of 1940 about 60, 000 Jews lived in Belgium. More than half these Jews survived the war. The Jewish Belgians survived for two reasons: first because of the efforts of non-Jewish Belgians and second because of the activities of Jewish underground groups (Yehuda Bauer, A History of the Holocaust, *260-62). "As of January 2002 a total of 1,322 Belgian citizens had been honored as Righteous Among the Nations at Yad Vashem in Jerusalem" (Martin Gilbert,* The Righteous, *294).*

— CHAPTER THIRTY-FOUR —

The Beginning of the End

My father had tried to get in touch with his cellmate, Mr. Demeer, who unfortunately had been deported to Germany. This was a terrible blow to his wife and daughter Jeanne, my schoolmate. Madame Demeer was a great woman, tiny in stature but possessing a sense of humor that was as big as a house. We all became good friends. My father and mother needed her for various tasks and she needed the boost my parents could give her, not only monetary but morale wise. I loved the way she talked and her strong convictions. My parents didn't always agree with her philosophy; she was a Communist and that was the reason her husband had been jailed. She and her daughter Jeanne were totally indoctrinated and we found out later that the party was helping them. Yet they never tried openly to convert us to their ideology but it was delightful to watch my conservative father rebut all her arguments.

Madame Demeer came from a background that was totally different from ours and she became especially fascinating to my mother. She could spend hours listening to Madame Demeer's tales. She came from a very poor family who had had a reverse of fortune and had been at the mercy of charitable organizations and public assistance. Madame D., only four feet tall, was certain that her height was the result of tests that had been performed on her in a public hospital. At the turn of the twentieth century welfare recipients couldn't afford doctors' fees and so had to be treated in public hospitals subsidized by the City of Brussels. She was positive that she had served as a guinea pig for the medical students who interned at that hospital when she was three or four years old. They had diagnosed her with a childhood disease. She was sure that the myriad of tests performed on her had stunted her growth. The rest of her family was of normal size, so was her daughter Jeanne, an incredibly good student. We found out later that the Communist party paid Jeanne's school tuition and even provided a piano so Jeanne could be proficient in music, a necessary talent if you desired to become a kindergarten teacher. At that time the USSR (the former Soviet Union) was our ally,[12] and Madame Demeer, who was collecting money for the wives and children of political prisoners, had asked my sister's assistance. At first my sister didn't know that the money collected was destined for the Communists, but as soon as she found out, she stopped. My father was as much anti-Communist as he was anti-Nazi; therefore, he asked my sister to desist. As for Mr. Demeer we never heard from him again; he never came back from the concentration camp where he had been sent and whose location was never divulged even to his widow. She told us that it was as if he had vanished in thin air.

— CHAPTER THIRTY-FIVE —

1944

During this tough and hard period we experienced some great moments; there was a profound bond between all of us. We regarded the war as the great equalizer with nobody pretending to be better than another, and the bond that existed gave us much love and confidence. We were still straining to listen to the BBC and the news started to get a little better. The allies claimed victories over the Germans in Africa. Oh . . . how elated and joyful we were. To show our solidarity on our lapels we wore a bit of green ribbon, green—the color of "hope." I still don't know how it came about and who started it, but those who had listened to the clandestine BBC broadcasts wore the bit of green acknowledging to each other that all was not lost. However, when the news didn't go our way and the allies had a reverse of fortune we all wore a bit of brown ribbon. I doubt if I have to give explicit reasons to our choosing brown. Draw your own conclusions.

The year 1944 was not a very good year for the Nazis. They were losing on every front and were now recruiting young Belgian civilians to work in ammunition factories in Germany. We were now in contact with the Belgian *Maquis*. My brother had vanished after telling my father that he was in contact with the underground, and with my parents blessing had rejoined his best friend in France. Although it was a very trying time for my parents, we never hesitated thinking positively and that everything would go according to his plans. We knew that after meeting his friend in France, they were both headed for Spain, Portugal, and England as their final destination.

Remember that teenagers, who had no value to the Germans when they invaded our country, had now become as precious as gold ingots. Those thirteen year olds had come of age and were being sent to Germany to work in terrible conditions. They were working in ammunition and military equipment factories that the allies were now bombing unmercifully. We lost several of our friends before we realized that it was time to protect our young boys.

It didn't take long for my father to shelter the two sons of one of his friends. Poucet and Milo, young strapping boys, had both been raised in the country, close to Brussels, and they replaced our Jewish tenants. Both were very healthy looking and were incredibly hungry most of the time. They were visited by their mother who would bring them the food we couldn't provide.

At that time the cooking had to be done at unusual hours. The Germans controlled the gas pressure so we received the gas haphazardly. We were forever turning the burners on and sniffing to find out if the gas pressure was on. As a matter of fact, we used to leave the burners on at around 6:00 PM and were ready to do the cooking as soon as we either smelled the gas or heard the gentle whistling it used to make. I had to peel mounds of potatoes for those boys and then had to manage the cooking during the minutes that the gas was allotted to us by the Nazis.

Because those boys hated to stay by themselves in the apartment, they used to come down and spend time with us. Poucet, a good-looking lad, admired my sister on whom he had a crush. He used to wear boots and sometimes would stick his trousers in them. He would adopt his British-gentleman mannerism with his pseudo "plus fours" he reinforced this look by smoking a pipe. The poor young man was dying to sit at the terrace of a café and drink a cool glass of beer. Even the diluted state of the Belgian beer made him drool. However, that was strictly *verboten;* it would have been too dangerous for him to be caught idly drinking beer all by himself. But one day he was able to convince my sister to accompany him, sheltering him so to speak, to the neighborhood café in order to quaff a cool one.

The boys' mother was a good woman, the motherly type. Her heart was as big as the bosom under which it was beating. She had a knack for discovering new ways to fight hunger and soon found out by researching our neighborhood that the corner bakery would lend their ovens and their kneading machines to anyone who would bring her own flour and yeast. That flour had been bought on the black market, but the baker wouldn't ask any questions.

"You bring your ingredients, we furnish the ovens." The baker would charge a fee for the use of his ovens and kneading machines. This was a great idea because then the baker's machine and oven didn't remain idle. That bakery was really a pastry shop before the war and had been closed since the occupation because white flour was non-existent on the open market. A bunch of women always baked their bread at the same time, which somehow was regulated by the baker and the availability of the gas pressure. My sister was invited to one of those parties and was rewarded generously for her efforts. It was one of those days when we forgot that we were at war. I guess the smell of the baking bread would have us joking around.

Food played a major role in our lives. Food was a favorite topic of conversation and the dreaming and planning of fabulous dinners kept us going for a while. We dreamed of drinking a cup of coffee accompanied by our rich and famous pastry. When rationing became drastic, we were at our wits' end to find something that would be sustaining and would tame the terrible hunger pains we were experiencing. Meat in particular was practically unavailable. Then out of the blue the Nazis gave us rationing stamps for fish.

That was rather strange since nobody had been permitted to fish in the North Sea since the beginning of the occupation. That sea had been mined and fishermen were not eager to fish in those troubled waters. Another anomaly was that banks of fish wouldn't ordinarily be so close to shore, but in this case fish swam close enough to be caught without endangering the fishermen. At first the rationing was meager. We were allotted just a few grams of fish per person to be purchased on Friday. A few weeks later the rations were doubled and it became my sister's job to deal with the fish, ironic because fish was not her favorite. This small fish, a species we had neither seen nor eaten before, looked like herring but had characteristics of mackerels. Nevertheless we developed a taste for that fish, and the women began swapping recipes like mad. The fish became so abundant that after three months we didn't need stamps anymore to get the fish.

We used to go to the fish market with a bucket to bring the fish home. We used to bake it, fry it, sauté it, pickle it, boil it, serve it *en gelee* (jellied), raw, and my favorite was *a la daube* (in a stew). There was no lemon available as a garnish, and no mayonnaise either. But everybody was eating fish and so much of it that for many it was a blessing. It replenished the calcium that we needed so much, it was rich in protein and loaded with good cholesterol; furthermore, it was delicious and the variety of ways it was presented made that fish palatable.

At that time the Nazis were also rationing water and men had to shave every other day. This prompted some comments from the men with five o'clock shadows, blaming it on the fish bones for giving their face that unkempt appearance. It is also strange to know that after the war that school of fish disappeared and we could never find that fish anymore. We called them "Manna from Heaven." Many argued that if we couldn't find that fish after the war it was because we were all sick of it or, as another would say, "We had other fish to fry." I still think that it was a miracle and many agree with me.

— CHAPTER THIRTY-SIX —

Home Worries

My mother was worried about something and I could not figure the cause of her short temper and worried look. Papa was acting strangely too. The two of them would whisper and even I, the oldest of the kids, was kept out of their conversations. Also my mother seemed to be gaining weight, something seemingly impossible in these times.

Moreover, Cilou, a young nurse, was visiting us frequently. We had become acquainted with Cilou when she was working for Social Services at my father's bank. She did the medical exams not only for their personnel but also for their families. The eldest of a family of fifteen, seven boys and eight girls, Cilou was engaged to a young man who had escaped Belgium and was now in the Royal Air Force. His name was Guy Webber. She was a tall, buxom, good-looking blonde who used to spend quite a lot of time at our house.

Her family lived in Waterloo on a very nice estate, where I loved to spend Sunday afternoons. The mother was a tiny woman, short and slender, who adored the only married daughter who had a little girl and was expecting another child. That little family was spending a lot of time at the parents' home. When I became acquainted with them I had met the sister's husband who was a mystery to me. He had a great sense of humor and Cilou tolerated him, although I thought he was lazy. I never determined what he did for a living.

Cilou's sister was protected by both parents and because of her condition was excluded from domestic chores. There were some younger daughters still at home and one son remained there too. Most of the sons had left home and were in a seminary somewhere in France. One daughter was in a convent as a postulant before becoming a nun. The parents were devout Catholics. The family used to go to mass every Sunday on orders from the father who himself abstained from church since Sunday was his day of rest.

The father, a gentleman farmer, owned quite a lot of land in and around Waterloo. He possessed a refined but rugged physique and wore plus fours and corduroy jacket with elbow patches, the uniform worn by country gentry. Waterloo is located in the French-speaking suburb of Brussels. There, the flat fields of Flanders are replaced by rolling hills; maples and oaks replace the cypress that border the Flanders roads; and the hills are dotted with big farms. Waterloo's historic flavor still inspires respect.[14] Wellington's Headquarters close to the main road stand guard, transporting one back to 1815. To think that Napoleon met his defeat there gives me the shivers. Although Napoleon was not a favorite of many Belgians, he was still a great general, a great strategist who was erroneously compared to Hitler. Hitler was a monster; Napoleon, a power hungry visionary, but certainly not a murderer like Hitler. I love Waterloo because that little village exudes the same energy that still prevails in Gettysburg, Pennsylvania. The two towns are similar not only in topography but also both are considered hallowed ground and revered in memory of the many who lost their battles there.

Cilou's father intimidated me a little; I could feel he was master and king of his domain. He was domineering—tall, rough looking, and taciturn. He was supposed to raise cows and sheep; however, I never saw him working with the animals. He had help, mainly the remaining son whose duty was to take the cows to pasture and bring them back at night. Monsieur was more of a supervisor than a worker. This would infuriate Cilou who would tell her young brother to leave the clan. She also convinced her younger sister to leave the convent; she was certain the poor girl had been forced by the parents to take the veil. In big families at that time it was a feather in the parents' caps to consecrate as many children as possible to Holy Orders.

Cilou became interested in communicating with the living and the dead by way of the OUIJA board. She wanted to find out the whereabouts of her fiancé. Unfortunately that source had dried up and wasn't responding to our exhortations anymore. We were now practicing the divining rod as a source of information. Cilou would hang a gold ring, a wedding band to be exact, to one of her hairs and suspend it above a world map. After being suspended for a while, the ring was supposed to swing back and forth like a pendulum above the country that was supposed to be harboring her beloved Guy.

We discovered he was in Africa, and we assumed the Belgian Congo. One day we learned that Cilou's married sister's husband had been mowed down by the Nazis for no reason at all; he had been shot while walking at the edge of some woods. We surmised that he was somewhat connected with the underground and now I could understand why he appeared so aloof. The Germans were now behaving irrationally, and we found out that a losing-the-war-Nazi was now an enraged Nazi. My friend Cilou still continued coming to the house quite frequently, and she became my confident. I tried to pump her about my mother's condition but about this she wouldn't tell me anything.

— CHAPTER THIRTY-SEVEN —

Philippe Arrives

Then one day my father broke the news to us while my mother was hiding in the kitchen. I believe this was one of the nicest things that happened to our family: my mother was expecting a baby in April. My sister and I were ecstatic—to my parents' delight.

By March of '44 there was little food available. Almost everything being produced in occupied Europe was sent to the Russian Front. We tried to get help from the Red Cross but my friend Cilou would give my mother some samples of food she would salvage from the Savings Bank pantry. My poor mother looked pathetic; the food situation was so disastrous she didn't gain much weight and could fit in her regular clothes for quite a while. Forget about maternity clothes, not in case of war. Then finally my brother Philippe was born on March 29, 1944.

He certainly wasn't overweight but he was healthy which is what mattered to us. He qualified to receive special coupons for whole milk and we took turns taking care of him. My mother's health was not great, so she had to return to the hospital for minor surgery. The Allies had resumed bombing Brussels; they would target railroad yards close to the center of town, but now our energies were directed toward Philippe and we felt quite protective toward our new baby brother. We would fight for the privilege of carrying him when we went to the hospital to visit my mother. During one of these outings the bombing was so severe that we had to leave our streetcar and find shelter in a bank. The ground shook so frightfully that plaster from the walls started to fall and a big piece of shrapnel fell through the glass dome above us shattering it into a million pieces but thankfully these didn't do us any harm. We were more concerned about the baby and about the sermon we would get from our parents for bringing the baby to the hospital to see my mother. The hospital was not close to our house and to get there was tedious.

It was terribly difficult if not impossible to buy baby clothes so we had to rely upon friends who possessed left over layettes, although believe it or not my mother still had baby clothes squirreled away from our babyhood. There is some superstitious thinking behind her frugality. It is said that in order not to get pregnant after the birth of a baby, keeping its clothes will prevent one from another pregnancy. We needed wool yarn to knit some baby sacques and booties for Philippe and once again the nuns from Bruges came to the rescue.

These were the same nuns who helped my father hide Jewish children. He would bring the children to them. In order to conceal their identities my father would lend the children his name, a name they would keep until the end of World War II.

The good sisters gave us some skeins of blue wool and we started knitting a few things for Philippe. The poor baby would be shivering in his high chair and telling us that his hands were freezing. My mother made my brother a little fur vest with the skins of the rabbits that papa was raising, which he wore inside the house to keep warm.

Philippe was precocious and talked clearly at an early age. We wrapped him up in the very famous *verte verte,* the blanket that had kept us warm during our aborted exodus to France in 1940, and kept my brother warm in prison, the first time, and still exists to this day. *Verte-verte* is now in my brother's possession and has become his own children's comfort and refuge.

— CHAPTER THIRTY-EIGHT —

Deliverance

In April 1944 fewer Nazis were around and the soldiers that occupied our country were not the young flamboyant youth that had come in the time of the invasion but old men, shuffling around in dirty uniforms. You could definitely feel that "times they were a-changin'." It also became easier to listen to the BBC; there was less interference and the signals were less garbled. We could feel that deliverance was afoot. We learned that my brother was in Ireland with the Free Belgian Army and that made us proud and happy to know that he was free and alive. We knew that before he left Belgium, my brother had been carrying weapons at some point and had been carrying them in his schoolbag on his way to school. Papa had found a Tommie gun between the rafters in the attic as well as munitions, which would have landed us in jail and shot immediately had the Nazis found them.

It was starting to be fascinating to listen to the BBC. The personal messages were not only numerous but cryptic at best. As I had explained before the "Personal Messages" were given during the BBC news bulletin, in the middle of the broadcast, and were coded. There was one especially that caught our attention. It was the first line of a poem written by one of my favorite French poet, Paul Verlaine: *"Les sanglots longs des violins de l'automne"* (the sobbing of the violins of autumn). That line was repeated over and over at every news bulletin and often with much emphasis by the anchorman.

The once proud Nazis started to look moth-eaten and shabby in their faded uniforms. We spotted Mrs. Heumann in the neighborhood and followed her to find out where she and the two girls were living. She didn't look happy, so we surmised that the husband was on the Russian Front. Papa, now a new father, was less boisterous and was uneasy about the future of the baby. But he rejoiced nevertheless at the turn of events.

Talk of invasion by the allies became more and more tangible and feasible. Optimism permeated the atmosphere, and we were even more disrespectful toward our enemy. We didn't fear them as much anymore because we sensed they had lost hope. The Allies were still bombing us, yet our prayers and good wishes went with them. The bombings were fierce, hitting their targets less randomly than before; many railroads had been hit with greater precision. The allies were definitely getting stronger; they had the equipment and gasoline. The German propaganda on the radio was also getting mean, trying to create dissention between the French and the English especially. One of their most detested slogans was the following: "The French give their chests, the English give their machines." This doesn't make much sense and loses its meaning in the translation, but the message was that the French gave their sons in exchange for the weapons from the English and Americans. That ugly little slogan didn't last long; even the Germans realized it was untrue and useless.

"The table is in the middle of the dining room" had now become the most repeated personal message during the BBC news bulletin. This had replaced Verlaine's poem, and the announcer's voice had an urgency that really intrigued us. We suffered less, knowing that the light at the end of the tunnel was peeking through. All of a sudden, hope for the future made life more bearable. Yet we still received bad news about some of our friends; they had been deported to Germany to work in the factories. That was hard on us because we knew those boys had been sent there against their wishes. They had been asked to report for a routine physical. The doctor giving the medical exams was Belgian; therefore, they had no fear. However, a few days later the same young men were sent to Germany not as prisoners but as factory workers. The ruthless Germans were still deporting people.

Our optimism grew day by day. We showed our hatred for the enemy openly, and they didn't seem to care anymore.

— CHAPTER THIRTY-NINE —

Darkness Before the Dawn

By April of 1944 the food situation had deteriorated drastically. All our provisions were about gone and my mother's health was not in great shape, but we had the baby to worry about and our main objective was to try to find ways and means to get nourishing food for him. We received some help from various organizations and neutral countries notably from Sweden, which would provide powdered milk for the children.

We knew the gasoline situation in Germany was deteriorating, yet we also heard terrible tales about a new weapon the Germans were developing. We were terrified by the enormity of the damage these weapons would inflict. Many dismissed the existence of these phantom weapons as being Nazi propaganda and classified them as mere gossip emanating from a wounded dragon, the last gasps of the mortally wounded beast. But we couldn't ignore what was being said. We also heard that the Germans had developed a tablet which when dropped in a bucket of water would become a gasoline replacement. Because we had been counting on a scarcity of gasoline, that little bit of gossip set us back. But we were more concerned about rumors we were hearing about the "secret weapon," which had become more tangible. Gossipers embellished the prowess and the deviltry of the unknown weapon and scared the daylights out of us. Moreover, we had had no further news from my brother. We prayed he was fine.

By May we mentally started to round up the traitors. We were making lists of people who had collaborated with the enemy. That new pastime kept us busy for a while. One of our friend's father's name came up quite frequently. He was the Belgian doctor, who was helping send our friends to Germany. We tucked all those bits of information in the corners of our brains, and we were already projecting ways and means to bring these traitors to justice—not necessarily the justice of the courts, but a more homemade justice that resembled lynching. Papa was especially bloodthirsty, a fact that surprised us since he was known to be quite the pacifist. But he let his imagination run wild as a kind of a diversion. As a matter of fact, we didn't know many collaborators; we trusted our friends implicitly.

I did have my eye on a Belgian woman taking my streetcar on my way to school every day. She was always accompanied my German officers, flirting with them. I knew she was Belgian because one day I purposely stepped on her foot to hear her yell in the language of her birth. She spewed her retorts in perfect French with the Brusselese flavor I was expecting to hear. This was not only a dead give away but it reinforced my knowledge of her **duplicity**. I profusely apologized to her and her escort, since I didn't want to end up in jail at this late date. No doubt about it: she was Belgian. I ignored her afterwards but kept my eye on her and made a mental note of her activities and tried to find out where she lived. She annoyed me because she was reading the _Brusseleer Zeitung_ (in German yet), the Nazi newspaper published in Brussels. This sickened me.

Then on June 4, 1944, the news bulletins from the BBC were interminable; the personal messages were urgent and frantic. Even the Nazis didn't bother to scramble them. We could hear them loud and clear. Our emotions were at their highest and the anticipation of a landing by the allied forces seemed to be imminent. The only deterrent was the weather. It was lousy, rainy and windy. Our hope was overwhelming when two days later it happened—D Day, June 6, 1944. Normandy was the landing place of choice.

To this day, as I am writing, tears of joy and gratitude come to my eyes. We cherished our allies and all of a sudden we realized the magnitude of those soldiers' sacrifices. We were elated but our joy was toned down by our realization that the German army was still a powerful enemy. To our immense relief, the liberating forces remained on French soil; they were not pushed back into the Atlantic Ocean. They advanced. They were fighting the great fight, they moved inch by inch but every inch counted. We were now glued to the BBC, which all of a sudden had become scrambled again. Rumors were flying but they were good rumors, even better than reality but we hung our hopes on every bit of news we could get.

People were giggling in the street, not loudly but discreetly so as not irritate our captors. Victory was in the air; we took our pain with patience. Marvelous visions of freedom but especially visions of food danced in our heads. When vacation time came at the end of June, we had time on our hands and tried to make the best of it.

Then one day we heard on the BBC that the secret weapon, which I mentioned above, was indeed real. They were being described as flying winged bombs trailing flames at their rear end. They could have been mistaken for a plane whose fuselage was on fire. They would make a pulsating noise as long as they were in the air but as soon as the noise stopped, the flying object would drop to the ground and explode causing a lot of damage. They were aimed at Great Britain and I believe some of them were launched from Antwerp. That fact was brought to our attention because to our immense joy allied bombings became more frequent.

Although the allied bombs caused a lot of damage, these bombings let us know that they were in control, that they had the resources, and that they were here. Days passed at a dizzying speed; the advance of the allies was incredible. Town after town fell under the allied power. It was magnificent to follow their carvings into Nazi territory. *Le General de Gaulle, le Grand Charles*, became our hero as well as General Montgomery, Monty, and our beloved Dwight Eisenhower, dear Ike. Then, on August 15, 1944, we heard of the patriot uprisings in Paris. This fact infuriated Hitler who demanded that Paris be burned to the ground. Four days later, Paris was delivered into the hands of the Allies. But the beautiful French capital was finally, if not officially, liberated on August 25, 1944. We heard by dribs and drabs that the Parisians were celebrating their deliverance with unbridled joy. The speed at which the allies were fighting and gaining ground was dizzying. The Belgians now clamored in the streets, naming the cities that were falling: "Did you hear? They have taken *Mons-Tournai*" (a region in Belgium near the French border). The allies were approaching the capital at the speed of light.

— CHAPTER FORTY —

The Retreat

Sunday, September 3, 1944, marked the real beginning of the end for us. The German army was retreating. All traffic in the capital was suspended. No streetcar was running. The atmosphere was heavy with anxiety and anticipation. We ventured to the corner of our avenue to peek at an army in total disarray, at the sight of the vanquished soldiers trying to get back any way possible to their fatherland. I felt ashamed for them. The most vivid memory that remains is the one of a poor Nazi pushing his motorcycle along the main road, direction Germany. He had run out of gas, we believed, and finding the effort futile and inefficient, he pointed his revolver at the gas tank, shot the machine, which exploded right in front of us.

Then the soldier rejoined another band of soldiers walking, head down, on the long way to the German border or more likely to link with their defeated regiment. I thought I would be exultant with joy at the sight of the proud army in defeat, and at the soldiers who were now wearing soiled uniforms and scruffy boots. But, in spite of myself, I felt the pain they must have felt and the shame they were experiencing. All of a sudden my hatred for them vanished, but not forever. But at that very moment that profound hatred was replaced by a short lived compassion. It felt good to regain a bit of my humanity even if it was only for a fleeting moment. There was of course a last gasp left in our captors. As a last resort they blew up the dome of our Palace of Justice, our Supreme Court Building. But the sight of the destruction, even though we lamented the fact that a historic monument was partially destroyed, was nothing to compare to the feeling of joy we experienced. Buildings can be restored to their past splendor. The sweet smell of liberty and freedom tickled our noses.

There was still madness in the belly of the beast. While we were smelling the sweet odor of coming freedom, a detached band of German soldiers started shooting at our dear Madame

Fourneau, the bakery lady, and her favorite customer, the retired priest, who used to voice his anti Nazi opinions openly.

However they did not die but were wounded seriously leaving Madame Fourneau to walk with a cane for the rest of her life. They remained very close, even closer than before, now bonded by their injuries and their hatred of the enemy. Madame Forneau had always been anticlerical but their common injuries made the previous arguments more civilized. I never remember seeing her in church though.

We were counting the minutes and constantly trying to find out what was really happening. Our only source of news was the radio but it was still under the Nazi control and it was not possible to hear the news bulletin in order to get the hang of the situation. The weather was beautiful—warm, balmy, and pleasant. The streetcars were not in service and many citizens remained at home impatient to know how well things were going. Although our parents had asked us to be prudent and not wander away from home we couldn't stay put. We roamed, explored, and talked to our friends who could not contain their optimism and joy. We went to bed that night with hope expecting to be liberated a few days later.

— CHAPTER FORTY-ONE —

They're Baaack!

However, at around one o'clock in the morning we were awakened by some thunderous noise coming from the main boulevard located at least a half a mile away. My parents rang our bedroom bell and from the joy in their voice we knew that the news were great. We all ran to the street, in our nightgown and robes, and witnessed the most grand spectacle: our neighbors had been unfurling flags, which were hanging at almost every window. We found out that many of our neighbors had been making these flags by dying and sewing up bed sheets, and those makeshift flags were now hanging from many windows, just flapping without the benefit of a mast. They were caught between the closed window and the sill. It was gorgeous, festive and uplifting. Strains of our national anthem were being played somewhere, but the most fantastic thing was the throng of liberated Belgians running in their nighties and slippers to welcome our beloved liberators. We were running too and then WE SAW THEM—our liberators, our beloved Tommies (British soldiers), riding in their tanks and trying to park them on an esplanade facing the National Rifle Shooting Galleries.

At 2:00 AM the soldiers were dead tired but the Belgians were just beginning their demonstrations of love and gratitude. Everyone was jubilant, strangers speaking to other strangers as though they had known each other for years. Children and adults were climbing on the tanks to kiss and thank our heroes. I believe this demonstration of love lasted until someone reminded us that the soldiers needed their well-deserved rest. We walked back home and to bed with visions of happiness but especially food dancing in our heads. We woke up early and pinched ourselves hoping that we had not dreamed what we had seen just a few hours before. After breakfast we rallied our friends and we all ran to the place where we had seen the tanks a few hours earlier. They were still there, magnificent, surrounded by a multitude of worshippers.

But then, a young man, in his early twenties, demanded retribution and incited the crowd to round up the traitors, the collaborators, and the Nazi sympathizers. He didn't have long to wait before men of all ages rallied around the self-proclaimed patriot and zeroed in on a house where a supposedly pro-Nazi had been living during the occupation. A small group of armed men broke down the front door and demanded the man of the house to come out, which he did without trouble. The young rabble-rouser was pushing the so-called traitor with his rifle aimed at his back and the terrified victim was following the orders willingly. As he was coming toward me I had a good look at his countenance. His arms raised above his head were shaking with fear and his face, as white as a sheet, showed disbelief and fright at what was going to happen. He was wearing house slippers and hadn't had a chance to slip on his jacket; he was in shirtsleeves and suspenders were holding his trousers. The man was looking around trying to find a friend, a redeemer, or anybody who would declare that we had no right to take the law into our hands. Alas to no avail. The crowd was as though it was made of stone, silent and menacing-looking. The looks on the faces around me had that blank expression of a mind that had been made up, advertising that there was no need to reason with them. They were not going to negotiate the man's fate with any one.

Another young man, armed with a rifle, stepped in front of the man and quietly shot him in the stomach. The man crumbled on the grass right in front of me, in silence but holding his midriff, which became bloody and gurgling. His already pale face became even whiter than before and the spectators ignored another man's request for an ambulance. I turned away from the heinous spectacle and ran back home knowing that what I had just witnessed was an act committed by people who were not above the Nazis' principles. I spent the rest of the day sick and disgusted with humanity but with an optimistic eye on the future. The next day our liberators were still parked on the esplanade and an insatiable crowd was still milling around asking for autographs from the soldiers who obliged with grace and kindness. We couldn't have enough of our allies. We showered them with so much love and gratitude that we were impeding their progress in continuing the fight with the retreating Germans. It is a well-known fact the reception of the Belgian crowd was so enthusiastic that it endangered the outcome of the next battle.

Our allies now occupied the buildings vacated by the Nazis, and the soldiers were now billeted in the barracks previously occupied by the Germans. It became our sacred duty to entertain our friends and it didn't take long for the families around my neighborhood to adopt their own Tommy. My mother used our last pound of white flour to bake a monster cake in honor of our Tommies.

— CHAPTER FORTY-TWO —

The War Continues

D ays of happiness followed days of joy although the war was still going on. However we were free to listen to the BBC without interference and to our own broadcasting system, which had been repossessed by the Belgians. Bloody battles were still being fought and news from the front was not always rosy. We retuned to school reluctantly and still afraid of the flying bombs the Germans were aiming at England. The V1 and V2s rockets would miss their targets and quite often would end their erratic flight somewhere above Belgium. We even found out those missiles were being sprung from Antwerp and quite often would pass over Brussels. We could see them at night by the flame at the end of their tails and the putt-putt noise they would make. Bulletins were issued on the radio asking the populace not to discuss the crash sites and the whereabouts of those flying bombs. Spies among us could help redirect the trajectory of the rockets and make them more deadly to the English. When one of those would be pass over us we would be silent listening intently to their putt-putt noise and breathing a sigh of relief when this noise faded away. However, if the sound stopped abruptly, we would hold our breath and count to three after which the explosion would occur. The interval between the stopping of the sound and the explosion was so short that it was not possible for anyone to take refuge in a shelter. I remember being in the street during the alert when a piece of a broken window fell on my arm and ripped the sleeve of my beautiful red leather raincoat, the last vestige of our days of affluence.

The very next day on my way to school in the streetcar, I heard two gentlemen discussing the whereabouts of the bomb that had exploded the previous night. I was astounded to hear my compatriots talking about what we had been asked to keep to ourselves. I was appalled and yet not being a timid and shy teenager, I couldn't resist the urge to tell the men to shut up and to remind them that their talk would endanger the whole country.

No need to tell you they didn't heed my advice and before resuming their talk, they looked at me with disdain and told me in no uncertain terms to mind my own business. I still tried to reason with them and even invited other citizens to rally to my cause. I was totally ignored and asked to shut up and get out of their way. I was fuming and before leaving the premise I called them traitors, spies, and Nazi sympathizers.

A few days later on my way to school I met the woman who used to make out with a German officer and now was being very friendly with an English officer. That sight burned me because I knew she was Belgian. Remember—I had previously kicked her in the shins in order to hear her yell at me in her native tongue, which incidentally was not only Belgian, but also more precisely Brusselese. I rose from my seat and looked down on her and asked what had happened to her German boyfriend and if she missed the German newspaper, *Brüsseler Zeitung,* she had been reading all those past years. My voice had reached an amazing crescendo and the fellow passengers could not ignore me. To my dismay they remained impassive and started to look intently through the window at the scenery outside, completely ignoring my plea for justice and blood. I was totally beside myself, here was a collaborator known by everyone on that streetcar, people who had witnessed her debauchery with the Nazis during the war and yet kept silent, refusing to help me to "citizen" arrest a traitor. Fortunately for everyone, my tram stop came up and I was obliged to leave the scene. However, the same scene was repeated the next day when I caught her again with the same gentleman, the British officer of the previous day. I was so mad at the other passengers for ignoring my quest, and as I was pointing and shaking my index finger at her with tears rolling down my cheeks some fine middle-aged man took pity on me and came to my rescue. He asked me to give him her name and address (which I ignored) and he would see that the traitor would be investigated.

We were still at war, and though we had been liberated, we still had to be suspicious of strangers among us. I made sure I would comply and a few days later, unbeknown to her I followed her to her home and was able to find out where she lived. I was anxious to meet her again; however, she must have known I was after her and because the next day she didn't appear on my streetcar and I never saw her again. She must have changed her schedule and I took advantage of her situation.

— CHAPTER FORTY-THREE —

Life Resumes

Of course, school resumed, and we returned to our daily routines with our hearts full of joy and gratitude. At the time of Liberation I was attending college; therefore, my time was less structured than when I attended high school. I had more free time and was less constrained by a strict schedule. My parents and we kids adopted English soldiers ("Tommies") who were billeted at a nearby barracks and many of our friends did the same because it was the patriotic thing to do. Our Tommy friends were mostly fathers who were missing their families and we tried to comfort them as much as possible. It was great to have them share our meager meals, since the food situation hadn't returned to normal. But the Tommies brought us some of their K rations, which contained food we hadn't eaten since 1940. We relished their content, consisting mainly of healthy food like sardines, some kind of sausage, a few cigarettes, and chocolate. Since Brussels had been liberated by the British, we had not yet met the Americans. They came later.

Our days were filled with unabashed joy and delight. We were free to think and say what was on our mind without fear of being sent to jail. The stores started to restock but it was an uphill task. The war was still on but the news was great. The allies were carving Germany into big pieces and gaining ground every day. However there were still fierce battles to be fought and we prayed for the allies' success. My brother had landed in Normandy with the Belgian Liberation Army and was now fighting in Germany. We had been reunited for just a few days. Then we wished him luck and Godspeed for the days ahead. The latest addition to the family had been a baby when my brother rejoined the Free

Belgians but now Philippe was 18 months old and had started to talk rather fluently. My brother Guy was enraptured by his little brother, who became a deterrent to his returning to fight.

The Germans were desperate, fighting with all their might against the well-oiled allied forces. The Nazis were literally running out of gas but still inflicting some hard blows to our liberators. The weather, uncooperative, gave the allies some hard times. The Germans were familiar with the terrain and the weather and thus had a small advantage. It became crucial for able young civilians to volunteer as hospital workers especially. My buddies became *brancardiers*, which meant they had the privilege of carrying wounded soldiers on their stretchers from the ambulances to the hospital. In September 1944, after the terrible battle of Arnhem in Holland, the hospital was swamped with soldiers who had been burnt during the conflict with the Germans. It was heart wrenching to see our dear Tommies in such terrible pain. It also became our duty to entertain the troops on the weekend. We would improvise little acts, singing songs, performing skits, well anything to bring a smile to the poor soldiers. Christmas time was nearing and a group of students decided to perform at the hospital a series of songs in English. There were long hours of rehearsal when my brother who was on furlough, my buddy Gaston, and I decided to sing an American song, whose title I forgot, but had to do with a porter, a chambermaid and another hotel employee.

The rehearsals went along very well, until the day of the performance. My brother started singing like a house afire, but all of a sudden was struck with stage fright. I became confused, and being somewhat absent minded I lost my footing, which made my brother giggle like a girl. Gaston seized the situation with gusto and started singing both my brother's and my part, even using my falsetto to fill in. Then poor Gaston caught our giggle fest, forgetting his lines, which were replaced by tra-la-las. During our production we were advised that the Nazis had regained some strength and were menacing us again. We were devastated and petrified.

On the Western front, the Battle of the Bulge in the Ardennes, Belgium, had started in the middle of December 1944. When asked to surrender Lt. General Anthony McAuliffe had declared "Aw, nuts." The inclement weather had cooperated with the Nazis. Intense snow and fog over the battlefield hampered the flight of allied airplanes. World War II relied a great deal on air power; now no planes were allowed to fly to bomb their targets. The names of the famous American generals such as McAuliffe, Montgomery, Ridgway, Patton, and Eisenhower were in our prayers. We cried, we prayed. Then we became silent, almost paralyzed with the fear of a Nazi re-occupation. Our world seemed to crumble. Finally the weather cleared. On January 28, 1945, the Germans were defeated. This battle was the largest land battle, in which the United States participated, of World War II. The Allies won; however, between 81,000 and 103, 000 Allied soldiers perished.

We were finally saved. Germany was squirming under the heel of the Allies. We drank the sweet juice of success and finally we met our other allies—the American GIs. After being acquainted with the dignified British soldiers, the Americans seemed like a breath of fresh air, so cool, so unsophisticated, and so natural.

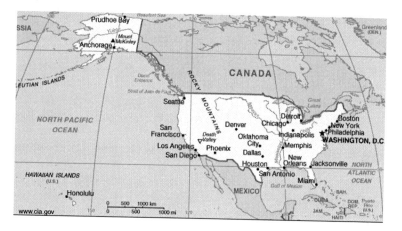

— CHAPTER FORTY-FOUR —

The Americans Arrive

Ginette and I belonged to an officers' club where we spent quite a bit of time. Strictly supervised, neither guests nor members were allowed to date the officers. We would dance the evening away, polishing our English. The experience we gathered was unique. We had had little contact with Americans before the war and meeting them was enchanting. They taught us how to jitterbug (frowned upon by my parents), but of course we had been quite acquainted with American Jazz and knew all the great Jazz musicians. Then actually to talk to them and flirt with them was magical.

We invited some GIs to dine at my home, to the delight of our parents who also found them unusual. It was rather surprising to find out that those young men who appeared rather aloof and full of life had a sentimental side. They missed home and many of our neighbors went out of their way to "adopt" their own GI.

We also learned many facets of American life, notably that when Americans wanted to go to the bathroom it was not to wash their hands. In Europe at that time a bathroom didn't contain a toilet; the toilet was located in separate rooms called the water closet or WC. When one of my GI friends asked to go to the bathroom, I assumed the young man wanted to wash his hands, upon which I took him to our bathroom and supervised the washing of the hands. I detected a desperate look on his face, but it never occurred to me that he just needed to pee. In retrospect, I am sure they considered me cruel. I remember vividly one GI pushing me out of the bathroom, closing the door behind me, and probably urinating in the bidet, a piece of plumbing the GIs were not acquainted with.

Another night my parents had invited a couple of Canadians for dinner. We were all having a good time, eating and drinking some vintage wine my father had saved for the occasion. One of the young men asked to be taken to the bathroom, which I dutifully did. Nothing unusual happened, the Canadian washed his hands, returned to the dining room table and left with his buddy around midnight. As we escorted the boys to the front door, they didn't linger as was the custom, no effusive good byes, no good night kisses. As they were swallowed by the night I noticed the seat of the pants of one of the boys. I told Ginette that it looked as if the poor guy had had an "accident."

The scene upstairs was rather unusual too. Silence hung heavily upon the scene. My father's astonished face and his request to my mother for a bucket of warm water and a washcloth confirmed my suspicion. The poor boy—in desperation—had let the floodgates loose. He never returned to my house again. However, it didn't take them long to understand that the bathroom, American Style, meant the toilet.

Another time a GI complimented my parents on their love of antiques and admired a credenza in the dining room, calling it a cabinet, which translated into French as the water closet. My father said seriously in the best English he could muster: "No, No, this is *not* the cabinet, the cabinet is in the hallway. This is a credenza. For pity's sake, I had a Canadian pee on one my chairs and now I don't want an American to poop in my credenza."

As days went delightfully by, our lives returned to normal. I had graduated from college and found a job as information hostess at an American base close to my house. I was well paid and had great opportunities to know Americans and admire the way they worked hard and endlessly. I also relished their sense of humor, which was less refined than British wit, which pleased us no end.

— CHAPTER FORTY-FIVE —

Retribution

After the allies had liberated the concentration camps, terrible stories of cruelty and massacre filled the news. We heard these reports on the radio and saw the pictures in newsreels at the cinema. Around this time we also found out some of our friends had indeed collaborated with the Nazis without us being aware of their transgressions. My friend, Jean Gregoire, who had worked with me in Louvain, rescuing Jews with Father Reynders, came back from the concentration camps, a shell of a man, walking with a limp and with the help of a cane. He vowed at that time he was going to Israel as a Zionist. And there were others who came back in pitiful condition, many of them wearing the striped prison suits they had worn in the labor camps. Those young people demanded justice and would sit on the stoop of the people who had denounced them to the Nazis. It didn't take long for the Belgian patriots to espouse their cause and ransack the house of the traitors under the gaze of the ex-prisoners.

My sister and I were friends with two young girls whose father was the turncoat doctor, who lived close to our house. One summer evening one of the girls, greatly agitated, came running to our house. She was terribly pale and could hardly speak, she was trembling so much. We tried to calm her down, trying to comprehend what she was telling us. Her father apparently had been accused of having worked for the Nazis, giving clean bills of health to the young men the Nazis had selected to work in ammunition factories in Germany. Many of those young men had perished in the bombing of those factories and the doctor was to blame. Our young friend begged me to come to her rescue, swearing that it was a mistake and that the people from the neighborhood who were trashing her house had been misled.

"My father is innocent, he is a humanist. Please tell those people to stop destroying my house." We had no reason to doubt her, since she and her sister were our patriotic buddies. I rushed to her house to witness a sad spectacle. The graceful French doors that opened to the paved courtyard had become an exit for the doctor's prize furniture. Everything was flying out—beautiful Louis XVI chairs, little side tables, and crystal vases. Exquisite bibelots were being tossed by the Belgian avengers under the scrutiny of an ex-prisoner wearing his stripes. Many of our neighbors were looking at the spectacle and giving a helping hand at either breaking the stuff or setting it on fire. I climbed the front steps, trying to avoid the flying objects, and made my plea, urging the populace to stop the carnage and attesting that the good doctor was totally innocent. There was a sudden hush hanging heavily upon the whole scene, the throwing of objects stopped for a second. Then the crowd started a crouching advance toward me, eyes squinting, fists clenched. Ah, but I wouldn't desist. At that time I pictured myself like Joan of Arc, carrying the flag and feeling seven feet tall. It was a proud moment in the life of a misled teenager.

All of a sudden, whose voice should resonate in the background? None other than my father's telling me to mind my own business and return home as fast as my legs could carry me. The crowd continued to eye me coldly but as my father made a gesture to grab me by my shirt collar and kick my butt toward the direction of my house, they understood. Papa was one of them. All that time my father had been part of the righteous citizens and had known all along that the doctor had been unpatriotic, to say the least. This little scene was repeated all over town, always under the vigilant eye of a prisoner, who made sure that no one absconded with the loot that was being tossed out of the windows.

— CHAPTER FORTY-SIX —

Boyfriends

At this time I met a young American lieutenant, graduate from Massachusetts Institute of Technology (MIT), who was my official "boy friend." He was my boss and we got along marvelously well. I excitedly told him about the autodafes, the burning of the traitor's stuff, and asked him to witness one scene happening nearby. Instead of rushing there with me, he told me in no uncertain terms that it was wrong, and that we had no right taking the law into our hands. I still wonder sometimes why the Belgian police didn't stop the pillaging and the torching of the people's possessions.

In the meantime, my sister, who was finishing high school, had met a young American lieutenant who had fallen madly in love with her. They had met at the Club and there was something incredibly cute about him. He was not too tall, had laughing brown eyes, and the most endearing dimples a man could sport without looking effeminate. The army officers' uniforms at that time looked spectacular. Their coat jackets were a dark green paired with beige trousers they called "pinks," and their kepis (caps with a brim), emblazoned with the American eagle, had the right shape and the perfect proportions. The flying air corpsmen also wore the most adorable furry boots in winter and OHHH, their windbreakers with their fur collars were to die for. Bob, my sister's beau, was in the Air Force (Army Air Corps, as it was called then), stationed near Brussels. The relationship was very serious and the young lad asked my father for my sister's hand in marriage.

The war in Europe had been won, but there was still fighting in the Pacific. My future brother-in-law wanted to marry my sister before his scheduled departure for the Pacific Theater of Operation. We all loved Bob who wanted to resume his studies at Stanford University upon his return to California and who told my father he intended for my sister to continue her education after their marriage. After a whirlwind courtship and many obstacles that had to be circumvented the lovely couple was married on August 8, 1945, in the sacristy of our neighborhood church. Then after the second Atomic bomb was dropped on Nagasaki, the Japanese surrendered and Bob was not dispatched to the Far East after all. Instead he was sent back to the US, leaving his bride in Belgium until the American Army sent for her. Finally on March 1946, she left Brussels for Paris accompanied by my mother.

War brides were extremely well treated by the American authorities, who were in charge of sending them stateside. They occupied very comfortable hotels. They let my mother stay with my sister to the great joy of both. My mother had mixed feelings and cried a lot upon her return to Brussels. After all, she was sending her youngest daughter far away to a country we knew little about. My sister was strikingly beautiful and her picture appeared in many newspapers and even on the newsreels of the day. Newspaper reporters made it a point to photograph her, and yet she seemed to be unaware of the waves she was making. She had a shy composure that betrayed her will to achieve what she wanted to accomplish. She kept a cool head in any situation and knew how to "defend herself," as my mother used to say. I believe it gave my mother the strength to let go of her at such an early age. The poor kid was only 19 years old, but her husband was incredibly mature and we trusted him.

After a brief stay in Paris, Ginette was sent to Le Havre, with the other War Brides, taking a ship to America in March 1946. I was very sad to see her go, yet at the same time I was very proud that my beloved sister had married an American. And a Californian no less.

California was across the world from us and my parents sometimes lost hope of ever seeing her again. Of course we corresponded tirelessly, and we received many packages from the United States. It was Christmas for us every time we received a parcel from Redwood City, where my sister started her American life.

True to his promise, my sister enrolled at San Mateo Junior College. She was immediately adopted by her new husband's family. To the delight of her mother-in-law who didn't have a daughter, they became fast friends and enjoyed doing "girl things" together, a treat for both of them. Ginette lived at the parents' home with Bob's two other brothers; one attended school with her. Her husband continued his studies at Stanford University, thanks to the GI Bill, and hoped to enter medical school the following year.[15]

I had stopped working for the Americans in May 1945 and was now employed by a laboratory doing secretarial work and going to journalism school at night. I met a nice young man at school, who was working for the soon-to-be Belgian Airlines, who convinced me that the future lay in the wild blue yonder. SABENA was hiring personnel and expected to resume their pre-war activities very soon. There was something magical about the airline industry in 1945. The pilots, hired by the Belgian Airlines, had been trained in England during the war and had escaped Belgium during the Nazi occupation, overcoming terrible odds trying to reach England. They spoke perfect English, sported great English tweed sports coats (they hadn't been issued uniforms yet and had permission to fly "in mufti"), smoked English cigarettes, and had adopted the British demeanor; in other words, they possessed everything that turned a simple man into a god.

I want to salute those war heroes who really stand in my mind: Captain Tabuteau, with the dreamy eyes and a smile to match, and Captain Andre Cohen, who had married an English girl while in England. Coco—as he was referred to—was loved by all. He was known for speaking with a lighted cigarette dangling from his lips, and when the ashes finally dropped after reaching a certain length and gravity intervened, he would not flick the ashes off his black jacket but would brush them off with both hands, making a terrible mess. But we thought it was cool; after all he also was a hero. Then there was Captain Paul Siroux, whose cute nose drove me wild. He was my pet, but far too sophisticated for me. I worshipped him from afar and when he finally couldn't ignore my antics to attract his attention and asked me out, I chickened out and refused his invitation, giving him the lame excuse that I had to baby-sit my baby brother. There was an aura about this man; his wife had left him while he was in training in England during the war and he was divorced, not common in Catholic Belgium at the time. It gave him that forbidden fruit appeal and yet created a need to console a man whose wife had betrayed him while away at war.

Captain Cocquyt, a World War I flying hero and a SABENA pilot from before the war, reclaimed his prior status and was rehired by SABENA as chief pilot and in charge of the flying personnel. All respected him not only because he had been a World War I flying ace but also because everyone knew he had been decorated by King Albert in 1918. He was a big man who rolled his r's and spoke French correctly but with a decidedly Flemish accent.

— CHAPTER FORTY-SEVEN —

Of Air Hostesses, Customs, and War Brides

E very young woman wanted to become an air hostess, but my father discouraged me from pursuing that route. I took and passed the test the SABENA, the Belgian Airline, was giving to prospective employees and was hired as a ground hostess. I would greet the passengers, direct them to wherever they were going, and give them the information they required.

I became a friend of the Customs inspectors and helped them expedite the influx of passengers through the clearing of baggage, which could be nerve wracking at times. However, I loved my job and never lost respect for those men who, in those days, could be **finicky** at best. I don't believe Custom Officers are known for their courtesy. They were rather short in their comments and were men of a few words, which were often spoken in a no nonsense voice. In fact they scared the daylights out of me. It was forbidden at that time to enter Belgium with alcohol whether declared or not. The authorities confiscated all alcohol passing through customs. But often after an especially arduous day the Custom Inspectors would summon me to their office where I would present myself shaking with fear and wondering what had I done now.

After making sure everyone heard their peremptory tone of voice and ordering me to come into their office, they would close the door after me and laughingly ask me to calm my fears and have one glass of the most delicious confiscated wine a fool had dared to bring in and drink to our good health. Thank you, Monsieur Verdefroid, wherever you may be. I avoided talking to my boss after the party with the custom officers, my breath didn't permit contact with anyone, and the scene was repeated each time a great vintage wine was seized by the "Border Patrol." It was only one glass of wine but it meant a lot to me: I was being trusted by the authorities.

Since I could speak English fluently it didn't take much time for the airline to send me to the United States to be a ground hostess and help passengers in distress who didn't understand either English or French. The German war brides had to reach the United States by the end of 1947. All airlines were expecting an onslaught and needed extra hands for processing the new citizens through customs and security. The poor German war brides, I am sure, had no idea of the monster they were about to meet upon their landing in the land of the free.

I landed at La Guardia Airport on October 7, 1947, on the most beautiful Indian summer day I had ever experienced. I stayed at the Barbizon Plaza for a few days, the guest of the Belgian Airlines, SABENA, and worked at La Guardia Airport. It didn't take me long to get acquainted with my new environment and the place that fascinated me most was the American drugstore. The concept of the "drug store" was totally new to me. I had never experienced such a setting. All the merchandise on display made me dizzy. It had been such a long time since I had seen such abundance. Yet I couldn't understand how people could eat in a glorified pharmacy surrounded by the smell of perfumes. I still carry that exotic smell in my nostrils, and love it. One of the rages at that time was nylon bristle hairbrushes, and I bought one with the thought of returning to Europe with a real trophy.

I was also fortunate to use the New York Independent Subway System to go to the airport, easy to use and rather direct. I had been told to stay away from the other subway lines, which were more complicated and less user friendly than the good old Independent Subway System. I had no problem dealing with dollars and cents, since our currency was also using base ten. However, it took me longer to adopt inches and yards and miles, but I still hoped for a change to the metric system some day. As for the temperature, I quickly figured out that you really freeze when the thermometer drops to 32 degrees Fahrenheit. I never used a conversion table. Hot and cold are easy to recognize!

After a week living in the lap of luxury in that nice hotel, I was asked to find some lodgings near La Guardia Airport. I was fortunate to find a room and bath with a nice family who took to me rather quickly. I could walk to the airport and started to enjoy my new work and my co-workers. I was replacing my friend Maggie Storm who had married an American and was now living somewhere else.

At first my job occupied all my time and it was fun to get acquainted not only with my American co-workers but also with the American way of life. I fell in love with American ice cream, which I had for breakfast, lunch and dinner. Besides chocolate, vanilla, pistachio, and strawberry, my tastes were rather limited, until the day I was confronted with chocolate mint ice cream. This seemed to me to be an aberration yet it was rather refreshing. After four long war years and that total lack of food, I was slender bordering on skinny and everyone was bound and determined to make me gain some weight. I didn't contradict my friends and took advantage of the abundance my new country had to offer.

My boss was Belgian but all the employees were Americans and I soon found out that my main job was to help the German war brides (Germans who married American soldiers) go through the formalities of the Security department and Customs. These young ladies were not very cooperative and gave the custom officers quite a hard time. There was a language barrier on both sides; therefore, I believe those girls felt they were in enemy territory. I had given someone the impression that I could understand German and my boss directed me to help the authorities as well as the war brides to go quickly through the formalities required by Customs and Security.

I was directed to step into the Customs Hall and the spectacle unfolding in front of my eyes was pitiful. There was total chaos. The baggage counters had been arranged to sport a different letter of the alphabet, and a huge letter was hung above the counter on a cardboard poster. These letters corresponded to the initial of each girl's last name, and each piece of luggage carried a tag imprinted with the girl's last name's initial. The only thing the girls had to do was to match the initial on their baggage with the poster bearing the initial of their last name, retrieve the baggage and reassemble all their pieces of luggage to permit the inspector to inquire about their contents. But the girls would not gather their baggage and would wait for the custom officer to do this for them. The brides were also reluctant to pay the Head Tax that was

imposed on every passenger in those days. To make them
understand that the two dollars that had been given them upon
leaving the *Faderland* had to be surrendered to the American
authorities was more than they could stand. It didn't take me long
to see what the problem was and how it could be solved. Now I
was in control! I did not speak German (my patriotism forbade
it), but I was endowed with a powerful voice. As I stepped into
the Customs Hall and yelled *"ACHTUNG,"* I could see the
frauleins (young women) all of a sudden straighten up almost
clicking their heels as they stood at attention. I mesmerized them.
I would scrape my brains in order to remember the few Flemish
words I used to know, and would demand those brides, in semi-
French and semi-Flemish, to immediately recognize their *Koffers*
(suitcases) and bring them together on the counter. To my
wonder, the girls did everything I told them to do, in silence and
with great dexterity. Many of those girls were married to
American GIs; some were only engaged; and many were pregnant.
I never smiled when talking to them and only referred to their
husband or boyfriend as their "lovers." The result of my
interference was magical. They were processed through customs
in record time.

SABENA, the Belgian Airlines, became the airline known for
the speed at which the German war brides were expedited. Not
only did they get through customs at record speed but also
security collected the Head Tax (a two dollar-fee) the brides were
reluctant to give up. That part of the procedure was easily
achieved. I knew the girls had been given two dollars before their
departure from Germany; therefore, I just grabbed the
pocketbook from the surprised woman, opened it up and ripped
the two dollars that were very often in full view. With a flourish I
would handle them to the grateful Security Officer. The other
airlines became envious of SABENA and wondered how the little
Belgian airline could process that flock of women at record speed.
When they found out I was the one responsible I became the pet
of American Overseas Airlines (AOA), Pan America Airways
(PAA), Air France, Royal Dutch Airlines (KLM), and even British
Overseas Airways Corporation (BOAC). They all begged me to
"speak German" to their war brides, a duty that I accomplished

with **alacrity** and joy. Revenge is a dish that should be eaten cold. It did do my heart good to see my old enemies taste the fruit of my discontent. However, all did not share these sentiments. After all the Belgian Airlines had been commissioned to gather the war brides through travel agents, and when the girls had reached their destinations, they complained bitterly to their husbands telling them they had been mishandled by a witch at the airport in New York. I was called by the sales promotion manager, who told me in no uncertain terms to stop immediately because it was going to cost SABENA its commission. I told him to mind his own business and I explained to him that I was helping the government of the United States. This didn't make an impression on him and I continued to act as I did before. Furthermore, that sales manager had a very sexy voice, and everyone around told me that he was incredibly good looking. I had never met him and in order to keep in contact with his sexy voice and his harsh criticisms I continued to harass the war brides.

I finally met him at the SABENA Christmas party. His being good looking was an understatement. He was incredibly good looking, tall, and lean; and when I met him and shook his hand, I made the most disgusting face I could invent. I was so smitten by him. His hair was parted on the side and his beautiful eyes didn't escape my inquiring glance. All the girls at the office had a crush on him, not only for his obvious good looks, but also for his **patrician** demeanor. He was very refined in his speech as well as in his manner. He would be classified as a "hunk" today. He was eight years older than I, and had seen more of the world than I had too. He had fought in the Pacific as a navigator on a "B" something plane. He was divorced. This alone gave him a certain *je ne sais quoi* (a quality that eludes description), an aura that was very American . . . Ah youth! Sweet youth!

— CHAPTER FORTY-EIGHT —

Marriage and Cape May

We fell in love. In December of 1947, Lance asked me to marry him as soon as I possibly could. However, my sister, in California was expecting her first baby and I had planned to visit her and spend a few days before and after the baby's birth. The timing couldn't have been worse. Snow was falling in New York City and didn't let up for two days. We were experiencing a blizzard of gigantic proportion. I was a bit reluctant to leave the east coast, and my new love was trying to convince me to stay. However, I had promised my sister and my parents to be with her so I flew from La Guardia to San Francisco on the last plane able to leave the airport in that famous blizzard of 1947-48.

California was wonderful. I didn't regret leaving the snow and the mess it had made behind. The kindness of the Californians and their acceptance of me were overwhelming. I fell in love with my sister's newfound family and all their friends. Ginette's mother-in-law was about my mother's age but less sophisticated. She had a special sense of humor plus she radiated a love of life that was contagious. She had had four sons but one had died during the war, and I admired the way she behaved with the three other sons who by the way were still at home. She had a knack of speaking to those young men and I envied her relaxed yet firm tone of voice when addressing them. The mother, Clara Belle, was not tall and sported the cutest dimples I had ever seen, giving her a forever smiling appeal.

We laughed all the time I was under their roof and we went sightseeing everyday. I was in awe of the wondrous sights California had to offer. I had never seen such vast scenery nor such towering trees. These plus the colors of the soft hills of the Golden State are forever etched in my mind. My sister had been attending San Mateo Junior College and I had a chance to spend a day with her at school. Since many young students had not met many French girls, I was surrounded by a bevy of adorable male students who tried their French on me. The weather added to my pleasure and if it hadn't been for the man of my life, I would have gladly planted myself in Redwood City. An arch at the entrance of the city proclaimed in no uncertain terms that "Redwood City: Climate best by government test." I believed it and still do.

Michele, my niece, was born January 15, 1948. By January 18, I was on my way back to New York City and my destiny. Things hadn't improved much in "the Big Apple" (New York City). Snow was everywhere, making travel difficult, and the day after my arrival I caught the flu and was bedridden for a few days. Time was running short, I had been slated to return home to Belgium; my visa was about to expire. By the time I was feeling fine I had decided to remain in America and marry Lance.

On January 31, 1948, the day before my scheduled return to Brussels, a justice of the peace in White Plains, New York, married us, and the next day we started apartment hunting. Since there were no apartments to be found, we stayed in a hotel and paid by the week. It was rather expensive and incredibly depressing for me to be staying in a gloomy room all day long. I had to give up my job at the airlines; at that time husbands and wives did not work for the same company—people worried about a conflict of interest. So I found a job as a French secretary.

My new husband's job demanded frequent absences required by his work with SABENA. However, after a few months of useless searching, we finally found a great place in Greenwich Village, between Sixth Avenue and Washington Square. Our apartment was the envy of our friends. We had six rooms and two fireplaces, a big antique kitchen, which I despised because it lacked all the divine features of my dream American kitchen. I especially remember the white and black tile linoleum that would not remain clean for more than a day. We had a built in cupboard that would be the envy of every antique dealer, but the sink was not built in, and although it was huge it had two separate faucets for the cold and hot water. A large window opened onto the gardens of the neighbors and gave a delightful view of the top of some mighty fine trees. I could hear the trickling fountain in the atrium of the huge building that abutted the house. I had heard that Mrs. Eleanor Roosevelt owned an apartment in that building, which she used as a *pied-a-terre* (a temporary or second place of lodging) when visiting New York. That fountain was the **bane** of my existence for a while; I couldn't listen to it without having to run to the bathroom. I wasn't feeling well and considered making a doctor's appointment. But first I had to find a job.

Because I had to resign from SABENA after my marriage to Lansing and to augment our income, I took a job as a translator in a firm importing veiling, lace, and ribbons from France. The store was located on West 38 Street in the garment district, and I loved the environment because it appealed to the feminine mystique—and to top it all I loved my bosses—three brothers who had respect and empathy for their employees. I remember one employee especially because he used to caress the material and lace that went through his fingers as he measured lace and women's hat veiling. However, the fountain in Mrs. Roosevelt's apartment and my more than occasional trips to the ladies' room made me suspect that everything was not all right. After a trip to the doctor, I discovered that indeed I was expecting a baby. Because at the beginning of the pregnancy I was often ill, I gave up my job; many women at this time did not work when they were pregnant. The attitudes about pregnancy were very different then. Indeed, pregnant women were not on television. Lucille Ball, of the *I Love Lucy Show*, was an exception and in December of 1952 when she remained on her show while she was pregnant, Lucy helped to change attitudes about pregnant women. (Even so the cast was not allowed to say the word *pregnant* on air.) So I decided not to work, but I had the brilliant idea of recommending my brother Guy for the job.

Guy was living in Brussels with my parents and working for Pan American Airways but my invitation to come to America soon won him over and he decided to see if my proposition to take my job was compatible with his working style. Guy had great references and so was hired by my firm, sight unseen. After a few weeks, my bosses became very fond of Guy and he became their right hand man.

In January 19, 1949, I gave birth to my daughter Leslie, and fifteen months later she was followed by my son Lansing II, which made my Belgian friends crack up laughing accusing me of wanting to establish a dynasty in a well established democracy.

Life in New York City was not fun for a young mother who craved fresh air, grass, birds, and flowers around her. Furthermore, now with a war in Korea my husband was afraid to be called to serve his country again. He said he would feel more secure if we moved into a community surrounded by all the things kids need and love. Finally after investigating properties in Connecticut and Westchester County, we realized that nothing was in our price range.

Furthermore my husband had some wild army friends living in Connecticut, and I decided that New Jersey was more in our range. For me New Jersey was "That State across the River." Little did I know it is a loooooong state and in order to confuse me even more, we started our hunt from the home of a friend who lived in Philadelphia. That is how I lost all my bearings.

I had no idea that instead of investigating properties close to the New York line we were driving away farther and farther south toward the delightful and enchanting Cape May County. We bought the first house we visited in Dennis Township, New Jersey. It was charming and had a past and character. The house had been moved back from the edge of the road on new foundations, and had the many conveniences I loved . . . except the kitchen. But the price was right and we now possessed land and a house. Ten acres to be precise. The setting was lovely. The property was located on a huge lawn and shaded by incredibly beautiful, old trees. We fell in love with that house immediately even before we found out that there was no way of commuting to New York City. Although the house had been remodeled, we did not have a gas or electric water heater. It used a bucket of coal a day, and coal was getting hard to find. But that did not deter us and the bucket-a-day didn't upset me too much because I had mastered the skill of building a fire during the war.

The New Jersey Turnpike was under construction, but the Garden State Parkway had not even entered the engineers' minds at the moment. Since Lance could not commute every day by train or car or even bus, he decided to stay in his mother's apartment and spend all his weekends in New Jersey. After learning to drive I would take him to Trenton every Monday morning, where he could take a train to New York City. He would return the same way every Friday evening. These were very hard times and I have to admit that it was sad for both of us to spend so much time away from each other. I used to cry on Monday morning, but after a while it became a routine.

I loved Cape May County and the way of life in the country, but I was feeling heartbroken when my husband took me to the General Store of the adjacent town to buy me a pair of "dungarees." They were flannel-lined. I also bought a flannel plaid shirt to go with the jeans. That outfit destroyed all my expectations and dreams of ever returning to the city. With all my might I hated wearing it. A few years later Dinah Shore sang a song that fitted my downcast spirit.[16]   The song was called "Buttons and Bows," which described how a cowgirl longs to wear pretty clothes, French perfume, buttons and bows; all that a city slicker is known for wearing.[17]

After a few years of commuting, we decided to return to New York City. My daughter was now ten years old and my son, nine years old. My brother-in-law had been assigned to spend a year in Greenland, which gave Ginette the opportunity to stay with us in New Jersey for the first six months and with my parents in Brussels for the next six months. She and her daughter decided to take our daughter Leslie with them—to my parents' delight. The happy trio left in August 1958 in time for the girls to attend school there. We missed Leslie terribly. That was when I decided to move back to New York City with our son and the cat, and of course to be with my husband. We were fortunate to find and rent an apartment on East 58th Street in Manhattan, New York, but kept our house in South Dennis as a vacation home. I also found out a few months later that I was expecting another baby. Gabrielle was born in New York City on January 14, 1960.

Afterwards we moved from New York City to Scarsdale, New York, where I taught French in a private school, but life was hard and too hectic and we all longed for the peace and quiet of our dear house. We returned to Cape May County in 1963, and the old routine started again but this time my husband's weekly commute was done by bus.

Although my life was busy taking care of my children, my old yearning to become a teacher started to dominate my few spare moments. Although I had been trained to teach in Belgium, my credentials did not correspond with the New Jersey Certification Requirements. I had to enroll in a nearby college, Glassboro State College (now Rowan University), to complete the curriculum demanded by the State of New Jersey. It took me six years to acquire my degree.

I was hired to teach in the Avalon Elementary School after having tasted the hardships of substituting. I taught sixth grade in the elementary school and used to tell my students about my adventures with the Nazis. They urged me to write a book about my life story during the war and all promised to buy a copy, except one child I had upset. She told me she would not buy my book, but would borrow it from the library.

And NOW, life is good.

Epilogue

This is the end of my story; however, I want to give a quick overview of the state of my life at the present time. My parents unfortunately do not belong to the living anymore; my father died in 1961 at age 63, and my mother died in 1984 at the age of 82.

My sister Ginette moved from California to Massachusetts in order to be closer when flying to Belgium, and my brother Guy remained in France after his transfer there by his firm. My brother Philippe born at the end of WW II works as an administrator for the European Council in Brussels, and he and his wife Cathy have adopted two Korean orphans. The older of the two, Onessa, studied Computer Animation for four years at the Ringling School of Design in Sarasota, Florida, and returning to Europe misses her adopted country very much

My daughter Leslie married her high school sweetheart when they were both attending Temple University in Philadelphia. Chuckie became a helicopter pilot and opted to go to Germany.

While serving in the army, Leslie gave birth to a little girl, born in Frankfurt, Germany. I believe my father turned over in his grave at this but I found it quite ironic.

At the same time I had a chance to become reacquainted with the German people. I met Germans who had also suffered during the Nazi regime and who had to keep quiet for fear of losing their lives. It was strange to see busloads of German tourists visiting the Nazi concentration camp in Dachau. A few months earlier while vacationing in Freeburg, Germany, with my mother and my then eleven-year-old daughter Gabrielle, I found out that although the hotel clerk treated my mother and me with courtesy, he had been discourteous to Gabrielle. I realized that his patronizing manner toward me was because my country had been defeated by Germany; on the other hand, the contempt he showed Gabrielle was because he was still feeling the shame of defeat. I also had the chance to tour the incredibly beautiful countryside of Germany. It was hard to comprehend how the Nazis could have acted with such cruelty when surrounded by such beauty.

Leslie is now living in Alabama with her two daughters and is a school nurse at Fort Rucher Helicopter Base, where Chuck had done his training to be a helicopter pilot. Sadly Chuck, at the age of forty-eight, had had a massive heart attack and died while stationed there. I miss dear Chuck.

My son, Lansing, is a musician who plays a mean guitar when he is not building houses in Pennsylvania. He has one daughter.

Gabrielle, the baby, a math professor at Cumberland County College in New Jersey, has two children living in Florida. Two summers ago she became the grandmother of an adorable baby boy, Chase.

As for my husband, Lance passed away in 1996, after suffering from emphysema. He had smoked for many years. I am very happy to say that none of my children smoke at the present time.

Vocabulary*

Alacrity speed or quickness; eagerness
Articulated consisting of segments held together by joints
Bane something that causes misery or death
Bibelots a small household ornament or decorative object
Billeted lodging for troops
Bode to indicate by signs
Collier one who delivers coal; a coal miner
Duplicity doubleness of thought, speech, or action; the belying of one's true intentions by deceptive words or action
Élan vigorous spirit or enthusiasm
Ersatz a usually artificial and inferior substitute or imitation
Eulogy a commendatory formal statement, often given at a funeral
Exhorted to urge by strong argument
Finicky extremely or excessively exacting or meticulous in taste or standards
Fodder something fed to domestic animals, especially coarse food for cattle or horses
Maelstrom a powerful often violent storm
Patrician a person of breeding and cultivation
Picayune of little value; petty
Rebut to contradict or oppose by formal legal argument or plea or during a debate
Shunt to turn off to one side; shift; divert
Straf to rake with fire at close range and especially with machine-gun fire from low-flying aircraft
Vicissitudes a difficulty or hardship attendant on a way of life

All definitions from Merriam-Webster Online

Notes

[1]During WW II people did not have televisions so they got their news from the newspapers and magazines or from newsreels that ran before the feature film.

[2] The fortified line on the French side was called the Maginot line. The Maginot Line was a line of defensive fortifications built before World War II to protect the eastern border of France. Both the Maginot Line and the German fortified line, the Siegfried line, were thought to be impregnable. However, both were easily outflanked.

[3] During World War II the German army invaded Belgium on May 10, 1940. After two weeks of increasingly desperate fighting which left the Belgian Army pinned in the northeast corner of the country, Leopold made the decision to

Leopold III

ask for an armistice, which was granted on May 28. His action incurred the violent disapproval of the Belgian people and brought accusations of treason. King Leopold rejected cooperation with the Nazis, refusing to administer Belgium in accordance with their dictates. Despite his defiance of the Germans, the Belgian government-in-exile in London refused to recognize his right to rule. The Germans held him under house arrest at the royal castle in Brussels.

Heinrich Himmler ordered King Leopold and his family deported to Germany under an SS armed guard. The Nazis held the family in a fort in Saxony during the winter of 1944-45, and then near Salzburg, Austria. They were freed by the U.S. Army in May of 1945.

After an investigation by the postwar government into his conduct during the war, a referendum was held. The Belgian people refused to allow Leopold to return to the throne. He was not even permitted to return to Belgium until 1950.

4 "Flanders Field" by John McCrae:

In Flanders fields the poppies blow
Between the crosses, row on row
That mark our place; and in the sky
The larks, still bravely singing, fly
Scarce heard amid the guns below.

We are the Dead. Short days ago
We lived, felt dawn, saw sunset glow,
Loved and were loved, and now we lie
In Flanders fields.

Take up our quarrel with the foe:
To you from failing hands we throw
The torch; be yours to hold it high.
If ye break faith with us who die
We shall not sleep, though poppies grow
In Flanders fields.

5 *Kraut* was an epithet used for the Germans, who ate sauerkraut.

6 NSKK began April 1, 1930 when the *National Sozialistischen Automobil Korps* (NSAK) was founded on the order of Martin Bormann to organize all members who owned a car or motorcycle in a single nation-wide unit. All commanders of NSAK were SA-officers but most of the regular members were not. Adolf Hühnlein was made commander of the NSAK and suggested renaming it to the NSKK, which was accepted by SA-leader, Ernst Röhm, who was in the process of reorganizing the SA. When Adolf Hitler became chancellor in 1933 the NSKK expanded to 30,000 members. After Röhm and the SA-leadership were murdered during the Night of Long Knives (June 30, 1934,) the Motor-SA became a part of the NSKK and it was made an independent organization. The NSKK took over all German motorclubs in September 1933 and expanded to 350,000 members. In 1939 the NSKK was made responsible for the

training of drivers for the army in the NSKK Motor Sports Schools. When the war broke out the NSKK provided transport for the construction of the Siegfried Line (the defenses along the western border), assisted in traffic control, pre and post military training, and assisted the armed forces with transport. (axishistory.com)

[7] *Maquis* originally referred to the Corsican underbrush where bandits were able to hide indefinitely from the police, but it later became a French and Belgium term for all underground activities between 1940-44 and in particular armed resistance.

[8] A dumbwaiter is a small elevator used for conveying food and dishes from one story of a building to another.

[9] Swing—jazz usually played by a large dance band and characterized by a steady lively rhythm, simple harmony, and a basic melody. Outlawed by the Germans during 1933-45 because they associated the music with African-Americans, a so-called inferior race.

[10] Reverend Bruno Reynders' journals, that can be found at the United States Holocaust Memorial Museum in Washington, DC, mention Arlette's father and his work hiding and transporting Jews to safety. Father Bruno, a Benedictine monk, saved 320 Jewish children by hiding them in various locations in Belgium. It took many non-Jews working together to save one Jew, according to Martin Gilbert in *The Righteous* (315).

[11] The word *spa*, an every day expression in English used to describe a place of relaxation, refers to that small Belgian town.

[12] After World War II from 1945 until the 1990s, Western Europe and the United States were not allies of the Soviet Union. They were engaged in the Cold War.

[13] Plus fours are loose sports knickers four inches longer than regular knickers that are gathered at the knee.

14 Waterloo, a town in Belgium, where Napoleon was defeated in 1815.

15 GI Bill of Rights "1.9 million servicemen were discharged from the Armed Forces in the first year following the end of WWII. The Serviceman's Readjustment Act or **_GI Bill of Rights_** was created by congress to help veterans assimilate back into the economy and postwar society. The GI Bill of rights helped veterans specifically by providing: one year of unemployment benefits, money for college tuition, special low interest loans for home purchases" (users.gloryroad.net).

16 "Dinah Shore ranks as one of the important on-air musical stars of the first two decades of television in the United States. Indeed from 1956 through 1963 there were few more well known TV personalities. More than any song she sang, Dinah Shore symbolized cheery optimism and Southern charm, most remembered for blowing a big kiss to viewers at the end of her 1950s variety show. As hostess, she sometimes danced and frequently participated in comedy skits, but was best loved as a smooth vocalist reminiscent of a style associated with the 1940s. Sponsored a golf tournament for women" (museum.tv/archives/shoredinah).

17 1948 - "Buttons and Bows" from *The Paleface*, Music and lyric by Ray Evans and Jay Livingston
> East is east and west is west
> And the wrong one I have chose
> Let's go where I'll keep on wearin'
> Those frills and flowers and buttons and bows
> Rings and things and buttons and bows
> Don't bury me in this prairie
> Take me where the cement grows
> Let's move down to some big town
> Where they love a gal by the cut o' her clothes
> And I'll stand out
> In buttons and bows
> I'll love you in buckskin

Or skirts that I've homespun
But I'll love ya' longer, stronger where
Yer friends don't tote a gun
My bones denounce the buckboard bounce
And the cactus hurts my toes
Let's vamoose where gals keep usin'
Those silks and satins and linen that shows
And I'm all yours in buttons and bows
Gimme eastern trimmin' where women are women
In high silk hose and peek-a-boo clothes
And French perfume that rocks the room
And I'm all yours in buttons and bows.